# Understanding
# Demonetization in India

# Understanding Demonetization in India

## A *Deft Stroke of Economic Policy*

Shrawan Kumar Singh

**BEP** BUSINESS EXPERT PRESS

First published in 2019 by
Business Expert Press, LLC
222 East 46th Street, New York, NY 10017
www.businessexpertpress.com

ISBN-13: 978-1-94999-105-5 (paperback)
ISBN-13: 978-1-94999-106-2 (e-book)

Business Expert Press Economics and Public Policy Collection

Collection ISSN: 2163-761X (print)
Collection ISSN: 2163-7628 (electronic)

Cover and interior design by S4Carlisle Publishing Services Private Ltd., Chennai, India

First edition: 2019

10 9 8 7 6 5 4 3 2 1

Printed in the United States of America.

# Abstract

India is in a monetary turmoil post the 8/11 demonetization. Per se, demonetization is a great step and has created a severe macroeconomic shock. It has led to a sharp contraction in money supply for a short period. Demonetization's proponents have contended that it would cleanse the economy of black money and make transactions more formal and digital, thus improving tax collection and enhancing long-term growth prospects. No matter how brilliant the solution, the implementation certainly could have been better. The measure was humungous in scale, cloaked in necessary secrecy and complex. The possible immediate and longer term effects of demonetization on the Indian economy are debatable. Whether one likes it or not, everyone agrees that demonetization was something utterly remarkable and its effectiveness would be talked about and studied by economists and policy makers for decades to come. Demonetization has proved enduringly popular, and it appears to have made only a minor dent in the GDP. It helped to add more people into the tax net. It has reduced the size of informal economy. With the increased use of digital payments, economic transactions become recorded. The effects of demonetization will vary by sector.

This book, which is divided into 15 chapters, has the objective of analyzing some of the implications of the "demonetization" exercise in India. These chapters pertain to examining the very concept, history, critique, impact on overall economy and black money, move toward less-cash economy and digitalization, government–RBI relation, along with an assessment of 2 years of demonetization. This book has argued the need to be cautious in moving to a less-cash economy, because the economy lacks the necessary financial infrastructure. Gradualism helps avoid excessive disruption and gives institutions and individuals time to adapt. It puts authorities in a position to make adjustments as issues arise. It would be prudent for the government to focus more on proper institutional reforms to address the issues.

# Keywords

demonetization; black money; corruption; tax evasion; digitalization; RBI; economic growth (GDP); informal sector; agriculture and MSMEs

# Contents

# Preface

Demonetization has brought momentous changes in the economy during the past 2 years. The various sectors of Indian economy are placed in a very complex environment. Business managers are constantly facing challenges emerging from the continuously evolving new scenario. Since the initiation of the process, the Indian economy is going through dynamic changes. There has been a structural shift in the field of trade, industry, and finance.

This book attempts to provide various nuances of demonetization. The need of the hour is to learn all the new policies, structures, measures, steps, and their implications. It is because of the importance of demonetization that various academic institutes/universities included the subject in their courses. Although some books have been written on the subject, this book stands out in terms of its scope and content as it provides an overview of the concept, history, critique, impact on overall economy and black money, move toward less-cash economy and digitalization, government–RBI relation, along with an assessment of 2 years of demonetization. All these have been compressed into fifteen chapters. The book has been designed keeping in view the interest of professionals, teachers, and students of business management, commerce, and economics as well as the general public. It may not be out of place to point out here that in the given situation of frequently changing economic, political, legal, and social phenomena, any work on this subject can be hardly up to date. In order to stimulate the reader's thought process, a critical approach has been adopted to explain the key concepts rather than a mere presentation of facts. Each chapter has been written in a lucid and user-friendly manner, making it interesting to read and easy to comprehend.

# Acknowledgments

I am indebted to everyone who has contributed to my understanding of the subject. Different views regarding the effectiveness or success/failure of demonetization have been conveyed through seminars, conferences, reports, magazines, and newspaper articles. It is needless to say that in writing this book I have drawn from some excellent literature on the subject from the writings of many scholars whose views I have incorporated in the book, and I would like to express my gratefulness to each of them for their unique perspective and expertise. The quality of this book is shared by all; however, for the errors and limitations, I alone am responsible. Writing a book has always been an arduous task that requires enormous perseverance, endurance, and sustained commitment over a long period. This book is a product of my experience over the past five and half decades of professional work as a teacher, trainer, and researcher. I am deeply obliged to numerous students, teachers, scholars, and practicing managers with whom I have had the privilege of interacting in my professional career. A special word of appreciation is due to my old friend Prof. D. P. S. Verma (Professor of Commerce, Delhi School of Economics, University of Delhi), who very kindly accepted my request, at a very short notice, for going through the entire manuscript, which helped me in improving the presentation and bringing it to its present format. I am deeply indebted to him, but I have not been able to find suitable words to express my sincere feelings for him. There is a long list of people to whom I am beholden for their encouragement during the completion of this book. However, I would like to mention Dr. Rabi Narayan Kar (Principal, Shyam Lal College, University of Delhi), Dr. Sunil Ashra (Professor of Economics, Management Development Institute (MDI), Gurugram), Dr. S. S. Khanka (Professor of Management, Delhi Technological University, East Campus, Delhi), Mr. Dhritman Gupta and Ms. Prachi Singh (Consultant, NITI Aayog, Delhi) for their support. Not least members of my family for their patience in dealing with the opportunity cost of my spending the time to complete this task.

A very special thanks goes to my brother (Shri Prithwi Raj Singh, Department of Commerce, Satyawati College, University of Delhi, Delhi) for his unstinted cooperation and support at all the stages of my academic career. In preparation of this book right from the very beginning, Mr. Manish Kumar Sharma has been a great source of strength in providing all the necessary secretarial assistance, and I express my special thanks to him. I would appreciate any comments, corrections, or suggestions from all quarters so that I can continue to improve this text in the years ahead. I eagerly look forward to receiving feedback at **sksingheco71@gmail .com**, for which I would be highly grateful.

Shrawan Kumar Singh
*New Delhi (India)*
*January 21, 2019*

# CHAPTER 1

# Introduction to Demonetization

Demonetization is an act of canceling the legal-tender status of a currency unit in circulation. India is not the only country to introduce demonetization, and it is not the first time India has done so. Countries across the globe have used demonetization at one time or other to control certain ailments in their economies. Demonetization is an extraordinary experiment in economic policy that raises social, political, and ethical questions. There are criticisms of and counterarguments to this move by the government.

Every economic policy has certain consequences, and predicting those consequences is not an easy task. Therefore, every economic policy needs to take into account some basic considerations, including

  I. A sound theory;
 II. A rationale underlying assumptions and the evidence for those assumptions;
III. Cost–benefit analysis, including accounting for systemic effects;
IV. Unintended consequences; and
 V. Learning from similar actions elsewhere.

Such processes are complex and must be guided by experts in economics, business, and technology coupled with experts in policy execution. The Indian experience holds four lessons for policy makers. There should have been a clear process for receiving professional expertise, data, and analysis and a mechanism for debate and discussion of the assumptions and the impact. In this context, it is important to remember that every policy decision involves trade-offs. A fact-based cost–benefit analysis is essential (Chakravorti 2017). The impact of a policy decision of this magnitude would take years to play out. But the move would still lay the foundation for a better tomorrow if the government followed up with some measures.

Delivering the I. G. Patel Memorial Lecture in December 2006, Dr. Manmohan Singh had opined that "economic policy-making has always involved political choices since it has political consequences. . . . It was not enough that the arguments were intellectually consistent or were mathematically tested. In a democracy, such choices had to be also politically defendable and acceptable" (Singh 2006). The effectiveness of policies ultimately depends on what people want, what they believe, and what they know about their environment (Chakravorti 2017).

From a macroeconomic perspective, the interplay of demonetization in relation to its targets and objectives is complex. A single policy instrument is deployed as a one-shot, unanticipated shock to attain multiple targets with its possible structural implications (Kohli 2018). Raghuram Rajan, in his book *I Do What I Do*, reveals he was against the idea of demonetization. Policies ought to be accompanied by a theory about the expected impact of the policy intervention. This translation mechanism itself relies on the assumption about how real people behave in response to a change in their environment. Advocating the abolition of physical currency in advanced economies, Prof. Kenneth Rogoff (2016) expressed reservations about the government's methods, stating that a more gradual phase-out of the large-denomination bills would have had a much less disruptive impact on an economy in which more than half of the population is unbanked. There were many problems with implementation that made this move fall short of expectations. There was a need to have almost a military-style remonetization effort.[1]

A lot has been written about demonetization, some of it on partisan lines. As with many major government programs in India, it was the prime minister himself who announced demonetization and acted as the policy's main advocate (Beyes and Bhattacharya 2016). Since then, demonetization has been the most discussed topic in the country. This is going to be a pain for forthcoming gain. This move will prove historical and the first bold step toward the need for a better understanding not only of the black economy but also of how the economy works, particularly the informal sector. Demonetization is a fundamental corrective to the economy, much like economic liberalization was in the early 1990s. With 86 percent of a country's legal tender becoming illegal, it is but expected that finding "a new level of equilibrium" would require time (Kapoor 2016). Demonetization has changed India, its people, politics, and the money game. India will be analyzed in terms of "before demonetization" (BD) and "after demonetization" (AD).[2]

The term *demonetization* has become much more than a household name. Demonetization is a generation's memorable experience and is going to be one of the economic events of the time. India's economic policies have always been unique and contextual. Almost everyone seems to have a view on it. The best and the brightest in the Indian economic firmament have also spoken, and some of them have taken rather hard positions (Nayak 2017b). There is no doubt that demonetization seemed like a political watershed. It is expected that a disruptive economic policy intervention will have some negative consequences in the short run. The stated objective of demonetization was to reduce the size and scope of the black economy, to increase digital transactions, and to bring all economic transactions into the open. The unstated objective was equally important: to create a new political discourse around economic reform and engage civil society in that process. It is now possible to suggest that all these objectives were met in different degrees. That the economy, or some sections of it, suffered a slowdown is the negative consequence against which the gains have to be measured (Baru 2017).

Demonetization has not been successful in achieving its publicly stated objectives. The efforts to digitize the economy extended to hard-to-reach populations. Far from curbing the black money, it has inflicted avoidable hardship on farmers, daily-wage laborers, and informal enterprises used to transacting in cash. Policy makers should be aware of the challenge of making everyday purchases cashless. The implementation of any policy in India remains a problem because it is the most diverse and populated country in the world.

## Political Gambling

Speaking to the Bharatiya Janata Party (BJP) members of Parliament (MPs) on December 16, 2016, the prime minister condemned the behavior of the opposition parties in Parliament, saying that while the government is working against corruption and black money, the opposition is defending the corrupt. He repeated this argument less than a month later when he was speaking at a conference in Bengaluru and called opponents of the policy "antinational" and "political worshippers of black money" (OECD 2016). He positioned himself as a strong leader willing to take bold decisions and committed to societal change. An even more powerful argument that the prime minister employed, however, was appealing to the patriotic sentiment, highlighting that the people of India had "made the world stand up and notice [their] historically inherent qualities of sacrifice, discipline, understanding and commitment to the nation" (Chengappa 2016).[3]

Many opposition parties specifically targeted the prime minister personally, alleging that demonetization was aimed primarily at undermining the opposition funding and, in turn, benefiting the BJP in the upcoming state-level elections. They also alleged that the information about the upcoming policy had been selectively leaked to key members of the BJP and their affiliates in the corporate sector. The evidence brought forward by the opposition during a seven-hour parliamentary debate to support their allegations, however, was largely anecdotal and appeared aimed at achieving political gains rather than making a credible argument for increased integrity in policy-making and governance. Public opinion on the policy became increasingly polarized. A large part of the country's population continued to support the initiative, hoping it would penalize "rich criminals" and "hoarders of illegitimate cash" (Beyes and Bhattacharya 2017).

Critics were disappointed because demonetization had no political fallout but entailed a very significant cost to the economy. There was a fall in the growth rate of the GDP, and jobs were lost in the informal sectors of the economy that were choked of liquidity. Ordinary citizens wasted time and energy standing in queues to get their own money back from the banks. Then there were the direct costs of printing new currency notes, distributing them, and recalibrating the banks' ATM machines.

Demonetization was ham-handed and riddled with avoidable administrative glitches. With some prominent exceptions, economists across the ideological spectrum were broadly negative about the move as an economic policy. Civil society groups also contended that the "war on black money" narrative was being used to forcibly and prematurely integrate rural India into techno-financial systems, not to fight corruption (Pandit 2016). Others raised doubts on the efficacy of the policy, noting that demonetization would not affect the holdings of those whose assets resided in tax havens, gold, or real estate (Beyes and Bhattacharya 2017).

The government took the battle to the opposition on the issue of demonetization. There is a big difference between the government and the opposition party on acting against black money. The BJP has taken a stand against black money, celebrating November 8, 2017, as anti-black money day, whereas the opposition parties observed it as a black day. The message to the people is clearly that the BJP wanted to end black money but that the opposition parties are only trying to claim political mileage.

The Congress party dubbed the demonetization initiative as "India's biggest scam." Further, the economic disruption adversely hit the job market. None of the objectives spelt out by the rolling out of the demonetization drive were achieved. According to critics, the demonetization exercise was a sheer failure. The campaign against black money and corruption was a nonstarter as it failed to acknowledge its source in the funding and functioning of political parties (Vembu 2017). Despite the official claim that stone pelting and protests had been reined in Kashmir, violence took place almost every day, with frequent encounters between the militants and the security forces.

According to the 2017 to 2018 Annual Report of the Reserve Bank of India (RBI), the total value of ₹ 15,417.93 billion specified bank notes (SBNs) demonetized currency worth ₹ 15,310.73 billion returned to the banking system. This means that almost all the cash (99.3 percent) has been deposited back in the banks. Initially, the government expected ₹ 3 to 4 lakh crore of black money to get extinguished outside the banking system post the demonetization exercise.[4] This led to a severe attack on the government from critics over the purpose of demonetization. The government countered that just because the money was back with the RBI it did not mean that black money hoarders had not been held accountable. With new bank deposits, a paper trail was created.

According to a survey by the C-Voter, the combined firepower of the opposition, media, tax evaders, black marketers, and intellectual apologists amounted to less than 20 percent disapproval of the scheme on demonetization.[5] However, the critics dismissed this survey by questioning the authenticity, methodology, and sample size. In its defense, the government argued that demonetization had to be planned on a need-to-know basis so as to avoid leaks. Secrecy and decisiveness were crucial to the success of the exercise. The object of the exercise had not been confiscation. The generation of black money in future would not vanish but would be more difficult. One of the objectives had been to move India away from being a high-cash economy. Critics accused the government of changing the narrative around demonetization as and when it suited them.

It is important to note that the narrative on demonetization has continued to evolve with the passage of time and the availability of quantifiable data. However, the tendency of most people to base their narrative on preconceived notions, political leanings, and existing prejudices and biases is hard to overcome. Analysts continue to evaluate the political implications of this unprecedented move, using every election, no matter how small or large, as a quasi-referendum on demonetization (Hattangadi and Kelkar 2017).

Gabriel Lenz, a political science professor (Berkeley, USA), stated in his book *Follow the Leader?* (2012) that "the voters don't choose between politicians based on policy stances; rather, voters appear to adopt the policies that their favorite politicians prefer." Another political scientist, Fareed Zakaria, quoting Lenz in his recent essay (2016), observed that gut decision and emotional appeal often trumped rational analysis in the choice of the favored political leader. Moreover, the voters seemed to follow rather blindly, adopting a particular politician's specific policies even if they knew little or nothing of that politician's overall ideology. So it appears that the voters first decide on a politician they like and then adopt his or her policies. According to Lenz, this implies that the politicians have considerable freedom in enacting policies without fear of electoral repercussions.

In this context, no single or simplistic narrative of demonetization can explain the impact on a large and diverse nation. Much like the six blind men in the parable trying to describe an elephant on the basis of the parts that they touched and felt, some analysts focus on the economic aspects, while others assess the political implications. Even within trade and commerce, the impact on the unorganized sector may be diametrically opposed to that on the organized sector. With markets trading higher than on November 8, 2016, it becomes almost impossible to assign a causative weightage to separate the global reflation narrative from the demonetization narrative (Hattangadi and Kelkar 2017).

Even on digital payments, demonetization did not seem to have provided a significant and sustained push. The 2018 Economic Survey suggested that demonetization helped increase India's tax base, in terms of taxpayers, and this might have played some role in the increase in the tax-to-GDP ratio over the last 2 years. However, demonetization's impact on boosting tax compliance is trickier to assess (Padmanabhan 2018). The expected economic gains from demonetization were questionable. If one takes the overall picture of the impact of demonetization on the Indian economy, the costs of demonetization seem to outweigh the benefits. In an editorial note, it was stated that the mainstream media has echoed the negative aspects of demonetization so much that there are no takers for the government's defense, which is unfair in itself.[6]

One can recall that the government had warned at the time of demonetization and again later at the time of the introduction of the Goods and Services Tax (GST) that the growth rate would suffer initially but then pick up gradually. Yet there is not even a token effort to see a possible silver lining. On balance, there is no cause for euphoria over the results of demonetization, but neither is it an entirely negative outcome; there are some clear positive strands too.[7] "The wisdom underlying demonetization is yet to be ascertained. Policy design is no easy task. A particular policy may have failed to achieve all its objectives, but the hope remains" (Dasgupta 2018). It must be remembered that no country has enacted a reform that would help cure all the problems. Whether the demonetization in India was a boon or a bane remains to be seen.

## Endnotes

1. Mukhopadhyay, P. 2018. "Barter Economy is Reborn in Villages as India Cancels Cash." https://blogs.wsj.com/indiarealtime/2016/11/18/barter-economy-is-reborn-in-villages-as-india-cancels-cash, (accessed August 13, 2018).

2. Shepard, W. 2017. "After day 50: The Results from India's Demonetization Campaign are in," https://www.forbes.com/sites/wadeshepard/2017/01/03/after-day-50-the-results-from-indias-demonetization-campaign-are-in/#4fcb2e6250d1, (accessed August 13, 2018).

3. Interview of the Year: Prime Minister Narendra Modi Exclusive, His First since Demonetization, *India Today*. https://www.indiatoday.in/magazine/cover-story/story/20170109-narendra-modi-black-money-demonetization-opposition-830098-2016-12-29, (accessed August 14, 2018).

4. *The Economic Times*, August 30, 2018.

5. "Over 80 Percent Don't Mind Inconvenience of Demonetisation, Says C-Voter Poll," *The Times of India*, November 23, 2016. https://timesofindia.indiatimes.com/india/Over-80-percent-dont-mind-inconvenience-of-demonetisation-says-C-Voter-poll/articleshow/55566700.cms, (accessed March 6, 2019).

6. Unfair to see only blues in demonetization, *The Free Press Journal*, September 2, 2017.

7. *Ibid.*

# CHAPTER 2

# Functions and Importance of Money

Money is used freely and widely in settlement of various economic transactions. Money has profound effects on jobs, incomes, and livelihoods and, hence, deserves greater understanding. People are so much accustomed to the use of money now that it is difficult to imagine a modern society without money. As such, this chapter explains various aspects of money.

## Barter Economy

Before the advent of money, the activity of exchange was carried out through the barter system. In a barter economy, direct exchange was very common. Goods were usually exchanged with goods. The barter system of exchange worked well so long as human wants were simple and limited in number. However, in course of time, human wants multiplied, which led to specialization of occupations. This resulted in a lot of difficulties for exchange through the barter system, such as lack of double coincidence of wants, which restricts the number of transactions; absence of common denominator of value; problem of storage of wealth; subdivision of goods; and obstacles in the way of large-scale production.

As the economies developed, people no longer bartered one good with another. Instead, they sold goods for money and then used the money to buy the goods they wished to have. At first glance, this seems to complicate rather than simplify matters, as it replaces one transaction with two. Actually, two monetary transactions are simpler than one barter transaction. The present-day money has passed through three stages: (i) metallic money, (ii) paper money, and (iii) credit money. The present inconvertible paper currency and other credit instruments acting as substitutes for legal money are only a recent development. In the olden days, commodities, notably silver and gold, were used as money. Subsequently, when paper money and checkable deposits were introduced, they were convertible into commodity money. Presently, however, everywhere in the world, money that is circulating is in the nature of a fiat money that is used and guaranteed by monetary authorities, without legal constraints.

## The Concept of Money

Money is anything that serves as a commonly accepted medium of exchange. Perfect acceptability and fixity of value in terms of the unit of account are together necessary and sufficient conditions for an asset to qualify as money. Some of the definitions given by the authors are too narrow while others are too broad depending on how substitutable different assets are for definitive money. Substitutability refers to liquidity, that is, convertible to definitive money. Thus, the most narrow money measure is the definitive money itself. A broad measure would include other assets that could be easily converted to cash. Those who emphasize the medium of exchange function define money more narrowly than those who emphasize the store of wealth or liquidity function.

## The Concept of "Near Money"

"Near money" refers to an asset that can be quickly converted into cash. It is also called quasi-money, which is noncash asset that is highly liquid. "Liquidity" is not an absolute term; the most we can say is that there are degrees of liquidity, with assets being arranged in descending order of liquidity, on the basis of two criteria: (i) "transferability" and (ii) "reversibility"—that is, transferable without any loss. Goods that have such characteristics and can be converted inexpensively to money are said to be "near monies." These goods include treasury bills, insurance policies with immediate cash value, and term deposits (certificates of deposit) at depository intermediaries. Technically, the near money is not cash or currency. Cash and currency are considered part of narrow money since they contain money in actual circulation. Near money is considered to be part of the broad money. The post-Keynesian economist Perry Mehrling categorically asserted that "always and everywhere monetary systems are hierarchical."[1]

## Kinds of Money

Money has had several incarnations. These have varied over time and space. Economists differentiate among three types of money: commodity money, fiat money, and bank money. At present, in India, money consists of coins, paper currency, and deposit/bank money.

I. **Coins:** It is a metallic money. The intrinsic value of a coin is now the least important thing about it.

II. **Fiat money:** Fiat money serves as a good currency and performs the roles that an economy needs of its monetary unit: storing value, providing a unit of account, and facilitating exchange. Most modern paper currencies are fiat currencies; they have no *intrinsic value* and are used solely as a means of payment. Paper money or coins are of little or no intrinsic value in themselves and not convertible into gold or silver, but are made a legal tender by a fiat (order) of the government. Fiat money is an intrinsically worthless object, such as paper money, that is deemed to be money by law. To place it into historical context, one could think of three phases of the development of money.

*First*, the commodity money itself was a valuable object, such as gold or silver.

*Second*, the paper money circulated, but this money was backed up by holdings of gold and indeed could be converted into gold at a fixed price at any time.

*Third*, the paper money circulated, but it was not backed up by anything other than the government's promise that it will refrain from printing too much money so as to make it worthless. Since the Bretton Woods (1945), almost all paper money is of this type. Money is an "IOU" ("I owe you") or a promissory note issued by the state, which everyone is willing to accept in discharge of any claim and is, in fact, obliged to do so by law. The modern payment system is a fiat money system. In India, the RBI has a monopoly on the right to issue currency. Modern money are merely pieces of paper that have no intrinsic value of their own. All paper currency is inconvertible. The age of commodity money gave way to the age of paper money. The use of paper currency has become widespread because it is a convenient medium of exchange. Currency is easily carried and stored. It can buy things. As long as people can pay their bills with currency, as long as it is accepted as a means of payment, it serves the function of money.

III.  **Deposit/bank money:** Bank money consists of the **book credit** that banks extend to their depositors. Any transactions made using **checks** drawn against the deposit held at any banks involve the use of bank money. It is not like a coin or currency note that can be passed on from one hand to another for a transfer of purchasing power. A deposit is merely an entity in the ledger of the bank to the credit of its holders. We treat only demand deposits of banks on which checks can be drawn as money. A payee can (legally) refuse to accept payment in a demand deposit (made through a check) and insist on payment in cash. This is because there is no guarantee that a check will be honored at the issuer's bank. This illustrates very well the truth of the statement that "money is what the public believes to be money." Most money today is bank money—checking deposits in a bank or other financial institutions. Today, there is rapid innovation in developing different forms of money.

The clearing house facility is of great importance for the successful working of bank money as a medium of exchange. Clearing arrangements greatly economize the use of cash, since the mutually offsetting transfers of funds among banks are settled merely through double entries in the books of the clearing house without any actual transfer of cash and since such transfers constitute a large bulk of total transfers executed through deposit money. Bank clearings facilitate transfers of funds quickly and safely, and at low cost. The advantages accrue to the users of checks. They encourage the use of bank money in place of currency. For businesses specially, quick clearings are very important as they affect the day-to-day cash flow or liquidity positions of the check-using firms.

All the three components (i.e., coins, currency, and deposit money) of present-day money have one feature in common. All of them are fiduciary (credit) money—the money that circulates on the basis of the trust commanded by its issuers. Looked at differently, the use of fiduciary money is highly economical: it releases precious metal embodied in coins under full-bodied metallic standards for nonmonetary uses.

IV.  **Electronic funds and electronic cash:** Electronic telecommunication breakthroughs have improved the efficiency of the payment system, reducing the time needed for clearing checks and the costs of paper flow for making payments. Transactions can now be settled and cleared with computers in electronic fund transfer systems, computerized payment clearing devices. These include debit cards for point-of-sale transfers and automated teller machines (ATMs). Finally, the electronic cash (or e-cash) is the digital cash employed to buy goods and services on the Internet. The e-cash is acquired by a consumer from the Internet bank and transferred to a merchant's computer when a purchase is made. An electronic check, involving the Internet banking, makes it possible for a consumers to pay bills by e-check over the Internet. Electronic checks significantly decrease the cost of transactions relative to the cost of paper checks. The developments in e-money are exciting and have led some commentators to talk about a "cashless economy."

A **cashless transaction** connotes an economic state whereby financial transactions are not conducted with money in the form of physical bank notes or coins, but rather through the transfer of digital information (usually an electronic representation of money) between the transacting parties. However, the focus is on an economy where cash is replaced by its digital equivalent—in other words, legal tender (money) exists, is recorded, and is exchanged only in an electronic digital form. The point to be noted is that "a cashless economy is a system where flow of cash or physical currency is non-existent and all monetary transactions are done electronically via internet enabled banking or wallets, and debit or credit cards, at most abolishing or at times reducing physical presence between two transacting parties. Such transactions can be purchases, bill and utility payments and clearances or transfers." The circulation of physical currency is minimal. India uses too much cash for transactions. In reality, a cashless society is unlikely. While the flow of paper in the payment system is likely to shrink, it is unlikely to disappear, particularly for small transactions.

## Functions of Money

According to an old adage, money is what money does. Thus, the importance of money lies in the functions it performs. Traditionally, money performs four basic functions, which are summed up in the following couplet: "Money is a matter of functions four: a medium, a measure, a standard, a store." Thus, these four key functions make money the most efficient means of payment. These are briefly described as follows:

I. **Medium of exchange:** Money eliminates the need for people to have a double coincidence of wants. Thus, money's basic function is to serve as a medium that enables the purchase and sale of goods and services. It is something the seller would accept from the buyer. Further, money is the vital lubricant that keeps an economy going and contributes to its gross domestic product.

II. **Unit of account:** Money is a common denominator of value. It serves a very useful purpose as a unit of measurement. The generally accepted practice of translating the value of all transactions, wealth, and debts into a single monetary unit of account measurement, such as a rupee, is a great convenience. The principle of rational allocation of resources cannot be applied in the absence of a common unit of measurement. A unit of account is a basic number in a counting system.

III. **Store of value:** Money is sometimes used as a *store of value*; it allows value to be held over time. In comparison with risky assets, money is *relatively riskless*. As Friedman points out, "Money is something more basic than a medium of transactions; it is something which enables people to separate the act of purchase from the act of sale." Money is an asset, or a thing of value that can be owned. In this way, money serves as a bridge from the present to the future, as money saved today implies shifting of purchasing power from the present to the future. Money is not the only store of value. Owning a house or a tract of land is also a way to store wealth. Therefore, *the store-of-value function of money is not a unique function of money.*

IV. **Standard of deferred payment:** Deferred payments are those that are postponed for the future. Money enables current transactions to be discharged in future. It facilitates exchange over time by providing a store of value and standard of deferred payment. With the expansion of trade and commerce based on credit, money has become a standard of deferred payments. If money is the standard for current prices, then it is also the standard for future payments based on these prices. But for money to function as a deferred payment standard; it must retain value; it must also store value.

**Static and Dynamic Functions**

According to Paul Einzig (1959), the functions of money may be classified into two broad categories—static and dynamic functions. By its static functions, money serves as a passive technical device ensuring a better operation of the economic system, without actively influencing its trends. By its dynamic functions, money tends to exert a powerful influence on the trends of the price level; on the volume of production, trade, and consumption; and on the distribution of wealth. It is capable of stimulating or holding up economic and social progress. It may even exert a decisive influence on the course of history and on the progress of civilization. Such effects are produced by its dynamic functions. If the role of money were confined to its static functions, monetary policy would be a comparatively simple matter.

The changes in the purchasing power of money affect its usefulness as a store of value and standard of deferred payment and, in turn, the individuals' willingness to hold money. Very high inflation rates are referred to as hyperinflation. With such a rapid inflation, households and firms refused to hold official money. For money to be acceptable as a medium of exchange, households and firms must believe that it has value and will be acceptable. Policy makers have significant concerns about maintaining the purchasing power of official money. The standard of deferred payment function of money refers merely to the practice of calculating debts in terms of the unit of account used for money. Money has value because people are willing to accept it in exchange for goods and services and payment of debts. Thus, despite the fact that money has no value as a commodity, it has value simply because others are willing to use it as a medium of exchange and store of value. Money also becomes a suitable store of wealth because of its widespread acceptability.

## Importance of Money

One cannot deny the importance of money because it is the most essential thing that people need. Money is probably the most remarkable instrument. It is the lifeblood of a modern economy. Without money, the economy cannot function smoothly. Just as the strength and vitality of a human body is judged by the amount of blood and its proper circulation, the strength and extent of development of an economy can be judged by the requisite supply and proper circulation of money in it. The significance of money, to a great extent, depends on and is derived from the various functions it performs. These are as follows:

I. The division of labor is possible. It has made specialization possible. In more developed economies, individuals rely on specialization, producing the goods or services for which they have relatively the best ability. Individuals then exchange or trade the goods or services they produce for those they need. If a furniture maker trades with a boat builder, they produce more and better furniture and boats, respectively, than if each produced both with no exchange.

II. The accumulation of wealth over periods that exceed a human lifetime is possible. Perhaps most important of all, it has hugely advanced.

III. There is potential for amicable interaction between people, to exchange ideas and money. To survive as such, and to prosper, a rational exchange of fruits of ideas is made possible through money.

IV. Money is an integral part of all modern economies. It allows the economy to operate more efficiently and hence improves the standard of living. To see why this is so, consider what life would be like without money. Moreover, by encouraging production and higher quality goods—and thus income—an economy's allowance for specialization and trade increases its citizens' standard of living.

V. Money plays a very active and highly important dynamic part in the economic system through its function of influencing the general level of prices. The effect of the trend of the general price level on the economic situation is apt to be considerable enough and may have far-reaching social and political consequences. Indeed, it may even affect the course of history. Money is a powerful factor that is liable to stimulate or hinder economic and cultural progress.

VI. Money in its international aspects tend to change balances of payments, domestic supplies of money, relative levels of interest rates, and trends of international movements of capital. These developments tend to influence monetary policy, which has adapted itself throughout the ages to the changing concept of money as well as to the changing monetary system.

In ordinary times, one doesn't notice money, because it just works. But when money is disrupted, the working of the market economy is disrupted. Money is the lubricant of the economy; a shock to the money supply disrupts the economy and could lead to recession. The significance of money in all walks of life is so immense that modern life without money cannot even be imagined. It has rightly been remarked that "money is a pivot around which all economic activities cluster."

## Money: Boon or Bane?

Money is not everything, yet it is the means to achieve happiness in life. The following are some of the major features of money that highlight its necessity:

I. Money is all about being self-dependent;
II. It is about no financial problem;
III. One can live life to the fullest;
IV. One is free to make one's decisions with money in hand;
V. One can offer a better life to one's family; and
VI. One can help others in times of need.

From these facts, one can say that money gives the right to do a lot of things, and that is why it is necessary to have the right amount of money. Money is perceived as either a boon or a bane, but sometimes it is both. Money is very important in one's life but is not everything.[2] It gives a sense of freedom and ownership. One feels that with money, one can own anything or put a price tag on anybody's services. Ownership of something means the total control of its existence from beginning to end. Not only the worth of money but also its importance has changed.

However, the problem is that people run after money. Even the wealthiest person will want more and will try ways to make money. No one is satisfied with what one has got, and hence, most of the peoples' time is wasted in thinking about how to increase wealth. They forget to enjoy their life and just focus on how to get money. So they explore ways to make money to continue and enjoy a better life and give precious time to the family. As a means, it is a good friend, but as the only goal, it becomes an enemy. Money is a good servant but a bad master: it is useful to satisfy one's need, but when it feeds one's greed, it will disturb life. Money also gives the idea that one is powerful and independent, blind to the fact that one lives in a world of interdependence. The awareness of dependence makes one humble. Due to the illusory notions of independence that it brings, money is considered a part of *maya* (mythical wealth). There are also those who blame money for all the ills of society. Not only does possessing money bring arrogance, rejecting it does, too.[3]

Invention of money has not proved to be an unmixed blessing as its use has become a source of so many evils. If money is not used properly, it can create havoc and may prove to be disastrous for humankind. In real life, however, money is seldom completely "neutral" for any length of time. As long as people have faith in the currency, a central bank can issue more of it. But if the RBI issues too much money, the value will go down, as with anything that has a higher supply than demand. So even though technically it can create money, the central bank cannot simply print money as it wants. Money is an extension of the free-market social order. An error in policy in the realm of money extends to the entire society.

Money has encouraged many kinds of antisocial activities. However, it cannot be denied that most of the evils arise because of an improper use of money; these are not evils of money itself. Hence, there is a greater need to use money as a faithful servant than to become slaves of money and invite trouble. It has been rightly remarked that money, which has been a source of so many blessings to humankind, becomes a source of peril and confusion unless there is control over it (Robertson 1922). Who knows what "money" will be in 50 years!

## Endnotes

1. Quoted in Sashi Sivramkrishna, *The Wire*, December 5, 2016.
2. *The Economic Times*, October 24, 2017.
3. *The Economic Times*, October 26, 2017.

# CHAPTER 3

# Demand for Money

The demand for money comes from the desire to hold liquid assets, of which money is the only perfect example. It may be noted that money is not demanded for its own sake but because it can be used to purchase economic goods and avail needed services. The behavior of individuals and businesses is important in deciding the level of money balances they wish to hold to understand the demand for money. The demand for money is a key variable to explain links among money, the financial system, output, and prices.

## Concept of Demand for Money

In economics, the demand for money is the desired holding of financial assets in the form of money: that is, cash or bank deposits rather than investments. Money is not desired for its own sake. Rather, people demand money because it serves indirectly as a lubricant to trade and exchange. Money serves many functions; the most obvious reason that households and businesses demand money (currency, checkable deposits, and other close substitutes) is for use in making transactions. To conduct everyday transactions, households and businesses require money to hold. Demand for money means the amount of money the public desires and is willing to hold at any point in time. Money is a stock variable. Money stock is the quantity of money at a point of time. As an asset, money is demanded because of the public desire to hold it. The motive for holding money and the time period for which it is held may differ from individual to individual.

Money is necessary to carry out transactions; in other words, it provides liquidity. This creates a trade-off between the liquidity advantage of holding money and the interest advantage of holding other assets. The demand for money is a result of this trade-off regarding the form in which a person's wealth should be held. Holding money entails some cost.

The cost of holding assets in the form of money is not the storage cost. Rather it is the *opportunity cost*—what the money could earn if it were converted into so-called earning assets, such as stocks and bonds, real estate, machines, consumer durables, and personal belongings. The return from stocks and bonds can be easily measured in terms of dividends and interest. The cost of holding money has commonly been approximated by the interest return on securities, such as stocks and bonds. The higher the interest return on securities, the higher the cost of holding money.

## Motives for Holding Money

There are five theories of demand for money[1]:

    I.  Fisher's Transactions Approach
   II.  Keynes' Theory of Liquidity Preference
  III.  Tobin Portfolio Approach
  IV.  Boumol's Inventory Approach
   V.  Friedman's Theory

As per these theories, the demand for money is affected by several factors. The way in which these factors affect money demand is usually explained in terms of three motives for demanding money:

    I.  The transactions,
   II.  The precautionary, and
  III.  The speculative motives.

Together, they provide good reasons for people to hold some money in their portfolio in spite of the opportunity cost of foregone interest. How much of income or resources will a person hold in the form of ready money (cash or non-interest-paying bank deposits), and how much will he part with or lend depends on what Keynes calls his "liquidity preference" for the demand for money to hold or the desire of the public to hold cash.

Keynes argued that there are three motives for holding money. First, individuals will demand money to finance their daily purchases of goods and services. This is known as the transactions motive. Second, people will demand money as a contingency against unforeseen expenditures.

This is known as the precautionary motive. Third, people will hold money as a store of wealth. This is known as the speculative motive.

Generally, the higher the income, the greater the demand for money for transactions purposes. However, some individuals place a high value on holding currency because it gives them anonymity. People who are involved in drug trade, tax evasion, and other illegal activities may value currency because cash transactions are difficult to trace. Hence, the demand for money may be affected by changes in the volume of illegal activity or the tax code. The transactions demand for money depends on the volume of transactions, which are directly related to the level of income and business.

A **precautionary** motive to hold money arises as people prefer to hold a little in reserve as a precaution against unforeseen contingencies—the desire to keep extra money in the case of an unforeseen situation. Money is held not only by individuals for precautionary purposes; similar motives for holding money are applicable to business firms. Precautionary demand is the demand for money people want in case of emergency. This demand is assumed to be positively related to income.

## Speculative Motive

Keynes hypothesized that individuals allocate their wealth between two assets—money and "bonds" (representing all other financial assets)—assuming that the expected return on bonds is determined by the interest rate on bonds adjusted for expectations of capital gains or losses. The demand for money balances is negatively related to the interest rate on non-money assets. The speculative demand for money is affected by expectations as to the future course of the prices of financial assets, and thus interest rates. This behavior is an example of a simplified portfolio allocation decision.

Friedman relied more generally on the determinants of asset demand that depends on permanent income, interest rate on money, interest rate on bonds, return on equities, rate of inflation, ratio of human-to-nonhuman wealth, and other factors. His analysis of demand for money is based on three important ideas:

I. Money is a "temporary abode" for generalized purchasing power and includes time deposits and assets not immediately available as a medium of exchange in his money demand function.

   II. The demand for money has a time dimension. The amount of money people wish to hold needs to be calculated as the amount of weeks or months of income held in the form of money.

  III. Money demand is a portfolio choice because people must choose between holding money, other financial assets, and physical goods.

Although most people prefer to hold a part of their assets in the form of money, no one would want to hold all of his or her assets in this form. All people must decide what part of their wealth, or income equivalent, they will hold as money and what part they will hold as so-called earning assets, such as securities (stocks and bonds), or directly usable items, such as house, car, appliances, and personal belongings. In making this decision, a person must balance the benefits of holding money (convenience and security) against the cost of holding money. An individual will choose to hold a greater proportion of his or her wealth in the form of money only if the added return outweighs the cost.

To *sum up* the discussion, it is important to note that the demand for money is not at all constant. There are quite a few factors that influence the demand for money:

    I. Interest rates
   II. Consumer spending
  III. Precautionary motives
  IV. Transaction costs for stocks and bonds
   V. Change in the general level of prices
  VI. International factors
 VII. Uncertainty about the future and future opportunities

## Demand for Money and Demonetization

In the context of demonetization in India, it is important to first understand what is it that cash does in the economy? There are broadly four kinds of transactions in the economy (Rao et al. 2016):

    I. Accounted transactions,
   II. Unaccounted transactions,

III.  Transactions that belong to the informal sector, and

IV.  Illegal transactions.

The first two categories relate to whether transactions and the corresponding incomes are reported for tax purposes or not. The third category would consist largely of agents who earn incomes below the exemption threshold and therefore do not have any tax liabilities. The uses that cash is put to for these various segments of the economy can be summarized in the form of Table 3.1. Finally, there would be demand for cash for illegal purposes, like bribes in elections, spending over sanctioned limits, dealings in crime, and corruption. Kavita Rao et al. (2016) study points out that if one takes a snapshot of the location of cash at any given point of time, it is difficult to predict what the breakup of the cash according to these categories would be, but it would be safe to say that each of these components would be represented in that snapshot.

*Table 3.1 Demand for cash by various agents in the economy*

| Description of the Activity | Unaccounted Transactions (legitimate transactions but not tax paid) | Illegal Transactions (corruption, crime, etc.) | Informal Sector Transactions | Accounted Transactions |
|---|---|---|---|---|
| Medium of exchange | Incomes are earned through exchanges in cash, payments are made in cash | Payments for crime | Incomes are earned in cash and spent in cash | |
| Store of value | Balances held in the interim until alternative investment options become available (there exist a number of instruments that yield better return than cash—real estate, lending in the unaccounted or informal sector, and so on.) | Balances held in the interim until alternative investment options become available (there exist a number of instruments that yield better return than cash—real estate, lending in the unaccounted or informal sector, and so on.) | Savings as well as precautionary purposes (as yet unbanked in the psychological sense) | For emergencies (precautionary demand for money) |

*Source*: Rao (2016).

The role of currency notes as a medium of exchange and as a store of value is very high for the common citizen of India, which is still predominantly unbanked. A document by the RBI, published in 2012, observed:

> Cash remains the predominant payment mode in the country. Reflecting this tendency, the value of banknotes and coins in circulation as a percentage of GDP (12.04 percent) is very high in the country when compared to other emerging markets, like Brazil, Mexico and Russia. The cash-to-GDP ratio in India has remained range-bound over the last three years. Similarly, the number of non-cash transactions per citizen is very low in India (6 transactions per inhabitant) when compared to other emerging markets. While no specific study has been carried out, the presence of a well established network of treasuries/currency chests and over 1,200 clearing houses across the country may have contributed to the slow turn around and adoption of modern electronic payment products.[2]

The continued relevance of currency notes as a medium of exchange and as a store of value is important for more than 90 percent of India's workforce who continue to earn their wages in cash. These consist of hundreds of millions of agriculture workers, construction workers, and so on. Cash is the bedrock of the lives of these people. Their daily subsistence depends on their cash being accepted as a medium of valid currency. They save their money in cash, which, as it grows, is stored in denominations of ₹ 500 and ₹ 1,000 notes. The vast majority of Indians earn in cash, transact in cash, and save in cash. Indeed India's cash-to-GDP ratio (an indicator of the amount of cash in the economy) is 12 to 13 percent: much higher. Money is, metaphorically, the blood that makes the economy live and function. India is a particularly cash-heavy economy, with almost 78 percent of all consumer payments being effected in cash.

In the aftermath of demonetization, a fresh question arises as to "who wants to hold cash?" It is simple common sense that everybody prefers to keep cash. If the cash holdings of an average Indian are far in excess of what he/she needs to buy, it creates problem for the RBI. In this context, Hyder and Khan (2016) have observed that some people intentionally hold cash balances, while the following category of people simply hold cash because they see no viable alternative:

   I. Persons who have never had a bank account—this continues across generations;

  II. Small farmers who really don't know any better;

 III. Shopkeepers who sell primarily for cash;

 IV. Large wholesalers (cotton, wheat, agriculture produce, gold traders, rural middlemen etc.); and

  V. The poor and lower-middle class who keep cash balances in case of emergencies.

Those people who intentionally hold cash balances are forced to deal in cash because either their underlying business is illegal, or the source of money is bribery or corruption. Such category of people are as follows:

    I. Petty officials in provincial and local governments (and public sector enterprises) who view bribes as innocuous "speed money";

   II. More senior government officials, who may expect suitcases of money;

  III. Smugglers who transact only in local currency or dollars;

  IV. Money changers—*hawala* transactions;

   V. Real estate developers;

  VI. Criminal gangs;

 VII. Terrorists of various kinds (like left-wing terrorists); and

VIII. Bollywood.

## Endnotes

1. Mukher, S. 2018. "Theories of Demand for Money." http://www .economicsdiscussion.net/money/top-5-theories-of-demand-for-money/10465, (accessed on August 17, 2018).

2. RBI: Payment System Draft Vision Document (2012–2015), June 27, 2012.

# CHAPTER 4

# Supply of Money

"Money supply" is the pool of liquid assets that can be used to make payments. The amount of money is determined through a complicated process involving the public, the depository financial institutions, and the central bank of the country. The financial market for securities and the demand for and supply of money are closely related. Public and private sector analysts have long monitored the changes in money supply because of its effects on the rate of interest, the price level, inflation, the exchange rate, and the business cycle.

In economics, money supply or money stock refers to the total amount of monetary assets available in an economy at a specific point of time. There are various concepts of money supply based on the variations in the assets included as money, ranging from narrow to broad, depending on how substitutable different assets are for definitive money. Substitutability in this case refers to liquidity, the cost at which an asset can be converted to definitive money. Supply of money in an economy at any point of time refers to the volume of money held by the households and firms for transactions and settlement of debts, which consists of currency and demand deposits. The most narrow money measure is definitive money itself, which is the conventional measure of money supply. A broad measure would include other assets that could be easily converted to cash.

## "Narrow" and "Broad" Money

Modern money has several components. Apart from just cash and coins, money also consists of deposits with the banks, both interest-free demand deposits and interest-bearing time deposits, such as fixed deposits. The different components of money can be aggregated in the order of liquidity. Since money is primarily used to settle the day-to-day transactions, it needs to be readily usable as a means of doing so. Clearly, cash and coins are the most liquid forms of money, since they can be used instantaneously and universally to settle unlimited transactions. The sum of currency in circulation and the demand deposits with banks are often termed as $M_1$, narrow money. Demand deposits, or accounts with banks, are also quite liquid as the depositor can write checks against them for settling daily transactions. Though they are  neither liquid nor instantly available as transaction-settling medium as $M_1$, and despite this, they are considered as money, since it will be available at some point, and very often, as in the case of a fixed deposit, can be converted to cash for some penalty. Usually, time deposits are much larger volume than both currency in circulation and demand deposits. The sum of $M_1$ and time deposits is called broad money.

## High-Powered Money

High-powered money (also called the monetary base) is the sum of the currency in circulation with the public and the cash reserves held by banks. It is called high-powered money because it forms the base on which money stock is created as a multiple. A part of the monetary base is held by banks as a cash reserve ratio (CRR), which is a fraction of the deposits created by the banking system. This proportion is determined by a country's central bank. The currency with the public is also a part of the monetary base because people do not hold all their wealth as cash and may deposit part of their cash holding into the banking system as demand deposits. This raises the cash assets of banks, which can again use a part of the additional cash receipts to create more demand deposits and thereby increase the supply of money in the system. The high-powered money is basic money; real money supply is something more, because the deposits with commercial banks have a multiplying effect as an outcome of the credit-creation process.

## Institutions Influencing Money Supply

Money supply with the public is influenced mainly by the central bank of the country and its commercial banks. Through its fiscal policy, the government also affects, to some extent, the supply of money.

# Central Bank

The central bank of the country (in India, the RBI) is the major source of money supply in the form of currency in circulation. The RBI is the note-issuing authority of the country. The RBI ensures availability of currency to meet the transaction needs of the economy. The total volume of money in the economy should be adequate to facilitate the various types of economic activities, such as production, distribution, and consumption.

Although the overall stock of money can be altered in various ways, in modern times it is very common that the stock of money available for transactions usually altered by monetizing government deficits. The stock of money in circulation or that available for transactions can be altered by using various ways of increasing the stock of money is by monetizing government deficits. The government borrows money from the RBI against government securities (g-secs), and the RBI prints new notes to finance such loan. The government pays its expenditures with this new cash, and money stock increases. The RBI can raise or lower the CRR[1] if it wants to decrease or increase the leverage that the commercial banks can exercise on their cash holdings. A lower CRR means that the same amount of cash can be used to finance the higher level of demand deposits. Another alternative to change the stock of money with the public is to use the open-market operations, in which the RBI can buy or sell its holdings of g secs and treasury bills (another form of government borrowing) to change the public's cash holding. A buy operation will increase the stock of money with the public, while a sell operation will mop up the cash in exchange for bonds.

# Commercial Banks

Commercial banks form the second most important source of money supply. The money that commercial banks supply is called credit money, bank money, or credit creation.

# Government and Money Supply

The government also affects the supply of money through its fiscal policy. Wherever the government imposes any tax or borrows from the public, it reduces the volume of the available money with the public. On the other hand, when the government finds that its income through taxation and public borrowings falls short of its expenditure, it borrows from the central bank (against its own securities) to pay off its creditors. Consequently, the availability of cash with the public and the banking system will increase. As the availability of cash with the public and the banking system changes, so does the economy's capacity to expand or reduce credit.

## Credit Creation

In a sense, the terms *credit, debt,* and *loan* are synonymous; credit or loan is the liability of the debtor and the asset of the bank. In the words of Newlyn (1978), "Credit creation refers to the power of commercial banks to expand secondary deposits either through the process of making loans or through investment in securities." The entire structure of banking is based on credit. Credit means getting the purchasing power (i.e., money) now by a promise to pay at some time in future. Bank credit means bank loans and advances. A bank keeps a certain proportion of its deposits as the minimum reserve for meeting the demand of the depositors and lends out the remaining excess reserve to earn an income. The bank loan is not paid directly to the borrower; it is only credited to his or her account with the bank; every bank loan creates an equivalent deposit in the bank. Thus, the credit creation results in multiple expansions of bank deposits. The term "creation" refers to the ability of the bank to expand deposits as a multiple of its reserves. This is the distinctive power of the banks to multiply loans and advances, and hence deposits. With a little cash in hand, the banks can create additional purchasing power to a considerable degree. It is because the multiple credit-creating power of the commercial banks has been aptly described by Sayers (1938) that banks are not merely purveyors of money but are, in a sense, the manufactures of money.

A bank differs from other financial institutions because it can create credit. This is because of the fact that demand deposits of the banks serve as the principal medium of exchange, and, in this way, the banks manage the payments system of the country. Demand deposits are an important constituent of money supply, and the expansion of demand deposits means the expansion of money supply.

# Process of Credit Creation

The process of credit creation begins with the banks lending money out of their primary deposits. The primary deposits are in the form of cash deposited in banks. After maintaining the required reserves, the bank can lend the remaining portion of the primary deposit. This can be illustrated by an example: Let us assume that an initial deposit of $1,000 is made. The bank keeps a certain percentage (say 10 percent) of the deposited amount as cash reserve and uses the rest for new loans or investments. The process would continue ad infinitum, depending on the reserve requirements, decreasing additional amounts per step. At the end of the process, the originally deposited amount of $1,000 will have induced a 10-fold increase in new deposits or, in other words, will have "created" additional money of $9,000 and led to an increase in the total money supply of $10,000. The ratio of increased bank money to increased reserves is called the money-supply multiplier and is calculated using the following formula:

$$dM = dCD \times (1/r)$$

where $dM$ is the total additional money supply, $dCD$ is the initial additional cash deposit, and $r$ is the share of the reserve requirements. In the above example, this gives:

$$10,000 = 1,000 \times (1/0.1)$$

The above formula indicates the maximum theoretical amount of additional money created within the banking system on the basis of an initial cash deposit. In practice, there are various factors that restrict credit and money expansion to a smaller amount. The credit control policy of the central bank is the major limitation on the part of commercial banks to create multiple expansion of credit.

# Measures of Money Supply in India

In India, the RBI has defined certain measures of money as part of its effort to estimate the effects of the money supply on prices and economic activities. RBI compiles and publishes four different money stock measures—$M_1$, $M_2$, $M_3$, and $M_4$.

$$M_1 = C + DD + OD$$

where C is the Currency held by the public, DD is the Demand deposits of banks, and OD is the Other deposits with the RBI.

$M_2 = M_1 +$ Saving deposits with post offices
$M_3 = M_1 +$ Time deposits with banks (C + DD + OD + TD)
$M_4 = M_3 +$ Total post office deposits.

In this measure, $M_1$ possesses the highest liquidity and is also known as "narrow money," and $M_3$ is commonly termed as "broad money." As the quantum of money stock available in the economy has an important bearing on all economic aggregates, the monetary policy seeks to control the stock of money so as to optimize the growth of national income along with the price stability. The data related to money measures in India is shown in Table 4.1.

Table 4.1 Money stock measures

| Item | Outstanding as on March 31/last reporting Fridays of the month/reporting Fridays (in billion) | |
|---|---|---|
| | 2017–18 | December 21, 2018 |
| | 1 | 2 |
| 1 Currency with the public (1.1 + 1.2 + 1.3 − 1.4) | 17,597.1 | 19,509.1 |
| 1.1 Notes in circulation | 18,037.0 | 20,041.8 |
| 1.2 Circulation of rupee coin | 249.1 | 249.5 |
| 1.3 Circulation of small coins | 7.4 | 7.4 |
| 1.4 Cash on hand with banks | 696.4 | 789.7 |
| 2 Deposit money of the public | 15,076.2 | 13,276.7 |
| 2.1 Demand deposits with banks | 14,837.1 | 13,026.0 |
| 2.2 "Other" deposits with reserve bank | 239.1 | 250.7 |

*Table 4.1* (*Continued*)

| Item | Outstanding as on March 31/last reporting Fridays of the month/reporting Fridays (in billion) | |
| --- | --- | --- |
| | 2017–18 | December 21, 2018 |
| | 1 | 2 |
| 3 $M_1$ (1 + 2) | 32,673.3 | 32,785.8 |
| 4 Post office saving bank deposits | 1,092.1 | 1,256.2 |
| 5 $M_2$ (3 + 4) | 33,765.4 | 34,042.0 |
| 6 Time deposits with banks | 106,952.6 | 112,710.3 |
| 7 $M_3$ (3 + 6) | 139,625.9 | 145,496.1 |
| 8 Total post office deposits | 3,008.1 | 3,372.6 |
| 9 $M_4$ (7 + 8) | 142,633.9 | 148,868.7 |

*Note*: For scheduled banks, March-end data pertain to the last reporting Friday. As for row 2.2, exclude balances held in IMF Account No.1, RBI employees' provident fund, pension fund, gratuity, and superannuation fund.

*Source*: RBI Bulletin, February 2019.

## Importance of Changes in Money Supply

The effect of the increase in money stock will be spread throughout the whole range of financial assets and interest rates. The supply of money in a modern economy and financial system is determined by three key factors:

I. **Open-market operations:** Here, the central bank buys government bonds, effectively creating money.
II. **The "reserve requirement" imposed on banks:** This is the percentage of deposits made by customers at the bank that it must keep hold of, rather than lending it out.
III. **Interest rates:** Here, the rate of interest will influence how many households and businesses are willing and able to borrow. Most money in a modern economy is created by the commercial bank lending, so the rate of interest ultimately does have a bearing on the supply of money.

Although a number of factors determine the money supply at any point in time, the central bank of a country has considerable control over the process and can offset or reinforce other forces that are changing the money supply. In fact, we can view monetary policy in terms of the central bank's control over the money supply and the influence that the money supply has on achieving the goals of economic stabilization.

## Supply of Money after Demonetization

In this context, it would be worthwhile to examine the money supply position after demonetization. After the old ₹ 500 and ₹ 1,000 notes were scrapped, and the new ₹ 500 and ₹ 2,000 notes got widely circulated in the market, money supply was expected to reduce in the short run. To the extent that black money (which is not counterfeit) does not reenter the system, the reserve money and, hence, the money supply will decrease. However, as the new notes gradually get circulated in the market and the mismatch gets corrected, money supply picks up.

The most basic thing for a modern market economy is the stability of the money supply. Demonetization has undermined this. It is generally accepted that money facilitates more trades and improves welfare than what is possible without it. Monetary theorists would call this as money being "essential" because the total set of allocations achievable with money is much bigger than the one achievable without money. While current markets in goods and services facilitate current consumption and investment, credit markets allow economic agents to smooth production and consumption over time. Therefore, a pervasive reduction in liquidity, however short term, is bound to adversely affect both current and future consumption and investment decisions.

Currency in circulation had contracted to almost half the level of note ban on high-value notes of ₹ 500 and ₹ 1,000, as was evident by December 30, 2016, the last day to surrender the extinguished money, when the cash in circulation amounted to ₹ 8.93 lakh crore.[2] The contractionary effect on money supply produced by demonetization has been reverberating across the economy. As an immediate reaction, there was a spike in various digital channels—Internet and mobile banking, cards, and other new platforms like UPI. Of late, the pace of the switch to digital transactions is slowing. Money supply growth has picked up. It has crossed the levels last seen before the note swap was enforced. According to the latest RBI data, people's demand for cash continues to rise compared to pre-demonetization level.

Currency held with the public is calculated after deducting cash with banks from the total currency in circulation. Currency with the People (CwP), or people's demand for cash, was 7 percent higher at ₹ 18.25 trillion at the end of April 2018 compared to ₹ 17 trillion at the beginning of November 2016. $M_3$, which is the broadest measure of liquidity in the monetary system, grew 13 percent in May 2018 to ₹ 140.3 trillion against ₹ 124 trillion prior to demonetization. $M_3$ includes the value of CwP, current and time deposits, as well as institutional money market funds and other liquid assets, along with deposits with post offices.[3] Demonetization has not been able to significantly bring down the circulation of high-denomination notes. In June 2018, the share of the new ₹ 500 and ₹ 2,000 notes was 80.17 percent.[4]

Several explanations are offered for this trend, though not all are willing to reject that the digitization of payments has not picked up. Some attribute the surge in cash to a revival in rural economic activity, which is predominantly cash based. Others believe the surge could be due to elections in various states in 2018. The election funding is still cash based. The growth in currency in circulation is likely to remain robust. This, in turn, would put pressure on bank deposits as the circulating cash represents a leakage from the banking system.[5]

Demonetization was expected to have a direct effect of reducing currency in circulation, especially in the short run. In other words, the monetary base was expected to decline. In the near term, this would almost certainly lead to a decline in economic activity. At the same time, the currency deposit ratio also goes down and the government's expectation is that this will lead to an increase in the money multiplier. The money multiplier in India currently stands at 5.8; that is, each rupee that goes back into the banking system increases the broad money supply by ₹ 5.80. If prices are sticky enough and the decline in the monetary base is more than offset by the increase in the money multiplier, it effectively amounts to an expansionary monetary policy. The degree of this depends on how proactive banks are in making loans with the new deposits. If the RBI and the banking system can engage in this successfully, then it would lead to a medium-term boost in economic growth. In fact, a lot depends on how crippling the short-run effects are—mainly the apparent freezing of entire local markets due to the lack of liquidity. Second, for the money multiplier to increase, the banking system needs to make loans. Financial inclusion involves providing people not just with bank accounts but also easy access to credit. In fact, the most significant barrier for informal firms is not corruption but borrowing constraints. A large fraction of lending in India, however, is passive—to government-supported enterprises, or as part of its various subsidized credit schemes (Chanda 2016).

## Endnotes

1. CRR is a certain minimum amount of deposit that the commercial banks have to hold as reserves with the RBI.
2. *The Economic Times*, March 1, 2018.
3. *Business Standard*, May 22, 2018.
4. *The Indian Express*, June 10 and August 30, 2018.
5. *The Economic Times*, March 15, 2018.

# CHAPTER 5

# Relationship between Money and Prices

The relationship between money and prices helps in understanding the changes in the value of money. The value of money differs from the value of other objects in one fundamental respect. That is, the value of money represents the general purchasing power or command over "things in general." High prices of other things are reflected in the low exchange value of money. Similarly, low prices of other things mean high exchange value of money. The value of money is, therefore, the reciprocal of the general price level (p) and can be expressed as 1/p. One of the basic problems is to identify the factors that determine the value of money or to explain the causes responsible for changes in the purchasing power of money. Regardless of the particular theoretical bent, almost all economists reason in terms of the quantity theory at times. What is the process that links the changes in the money supply to economic activity? This chapter explains the underlying process that links the monetary and real sectors of the economy.

## Theoretical Approaches

The association between money and prices is expressed in the first crude version of the Quantity Theory of Money (QTM), which stated that the general price level is directly proportional to the quantity of money in existence. The QTM has a long history. The theory was rejected in the 1930s as a result of its failure of the conditions prevailing at the time. In the post-Keynesian era, it was restated by Friedman. A new quantity theory emerged in the late 1950s, and out of it developed the new economic school of thought called the "Monetarists."

With the onset of the Great Depression in 1929, the quantity theory was discredited by many economists, who considered monetary policy ineffective. The quantity equations are in no sense the ultimate determinants of the prices level. Instead, they are themselves determined by a host of psychological, technical, institutional, and economic factors. Thus, the ultimate determinants of the value of money are to be found behind the quantity equations. It means that the quantity equations are too general and include too little. They conceal offsetting changes in particular sectors. The quantity theory is treated only as an imperfect and unreliable explanation of money value. It does not give any precise clue to the causal process by which the value of money is determined. None of the quantity equations shows how an increase or decrease in the quantity of money reacts upon the price level. The omission of the *rate of interest* as a link between money and prices is a grave defect of the equation of the quantity theory. Quantity equations indicate the result, but they do not indicate the process of the result. Thus, quantity equations are less analytical and, therefore, less practicable. The value of money is a consequence of income rather than the quantity of money. Hence, it has been remarked that "quantity equations remain the most illuminating summary of the forces determining the general level of prices or the value of money." We may, however, conclude with Samuelson (2010) that "the quantity theory is over-simplified. But in times of inflation it comes into its own; and in these times it is so important that we should preach the quantity theory, in season and out of season."

## Keynes's Theory of Money and Prices

Keynes tries to tackle the problem in his general theory by a restatement of the quantity theory. In doing so, he tries to integrate the theory of money with the theory of employment. Keynes enunciated the QTM as follows: "So long as there is unemployment, employment will change in the same proportion as the quantity of money." According to Keynes, the primary effect of a change in the quantity of money on the quantum of effective demand is through its influence on the rate of interest. The immediate effect of an increase in the quantity of money is to lower the rate of interest by increasing the supply of money available for speculative motives (under the liquidity preference schedule of the community). A fall in the rate of interest, thus, brings about an increase in the level of investment (i.e., investment function constituting the effective demand rises because, given the marginal efficiency of capital, a reduction in the rate of interest will cause an increase in the rate of investment). An increase in investment through the multiplier effect on demand as a whole (i.e., consumption expenditures plus investment expenditures); leads to rise in employment, output, and income. In short, the general level of prices will not rise as output increases on account of increase in money supply, so long as there are efficient unemployed resources of every type available. But as output increases, a series of bottlenecks will be successively reached, where the supply of particular commodities ceases to be elastic and their prices will tend to rise sharply.

This is how Keynes maintains that changes in the quantity of money do bring about changes in the price level or the value of money not directly but indirectly, through affecting other elements, and that the theory of money is a part of the general theory of value. The key proposition of Keynes's monetary theory is that changes in the demand or supply of money (and both can change) operate on the level of economic activity not directly (as in the QTM) but indirectly through changes in the rate of interest and thereby through changes in real investment in the economy. The main propositions are as follows:

1. The rate of interest (r) is determined by the demand for and the supply of money.
2. The r determines investment (I) via the investment demand function.
3. The I influences income (Y) via the multiplier.
4. The Y determines the level of employment via the aggregate production function.

Thus, the influences of M on P are seen to emerge at the end of a long sequence of relations and effects. According to Keynes, the relation between M and P is not as simple as the QTM makes it out to be. It is established through a long chain of causation as shown below:

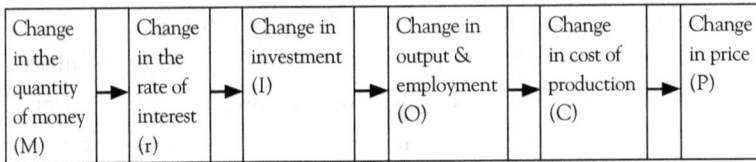

| Change in the quantity of money (M) | | Change in the rate of interest (r) | | Change in investment (I) | | Change in output & employment (O) | | Change in cost of production (C) | | Change in price (P) |
|---|---|---|---|---|---|---|---|---|---|---|

Keynes's restatement of the quantity theory marks a great *improve-ment* in the sense that he views the role of money in the causal process via consumption, investment, liquidity preference, rate of interest, etc. By reformulating the QTM, he conveys that there is the extreme complexity of the relationship between prices and the quantity of money in contrast to the simple immediate relationship exposed in the quantity equations given by Fisher and the Cambridge economists. Moreover, Keynes's great merit lies in integrating the theory of money with the theory of value. Thus, Keynes in his restatement of the theory provided the missing link in the old QTM. Even the leading modern quantity theorist Professor Friedman has admitted that the relation between M and P is quite loose and undependable, as several things relating the two can change from time to time. Friedman reformulated the quantity theory to determine the quantity of money that people desire to hold.

## Evaluation of Different Approaches

QTM refers to the proposition that changes in the quantity of money lead to, other factors remaining constant, approximately equal changes in the price level. The theory is derived from an accounting identity, according to which the total expenditures in the economy (MV) are identical to total receipts from the sale of final goods and services (PY). The advent of Keynesian economics in the 1930s rendered the QTM of minor importance, and it was used only for the determination of nominal magnitudes of real variables. According to Keynesian analysis, the quantity of money could not affect the real economy in any direct way but only indirectly through variations in the interest rate.

In contrast, Friedman claimed that money matters and is responsible for almost every economic phenomenon. Friedman views the money demand function as stable. Money, like any other goods, has attributes that make it useful. Friedman includes separate yields for bonds, equities, and durable goods. Friedman makes explicit the possibility of other substitutions and also allows for a shift from money directly into commodities (durable goods) as rates of return change. The effect of money supply on prices may work indirectly through variations in interest rates, which in turn induce effects on aggregate demand. The empirical evidence with respect to the effects of the money supply on the price level so far has been mixed and depends on the definitions of the money supply (narrow or broad) and the time period. Friedman's analysis reveals that the relationship between the demand for money and interest rates is weak. This weak relationship results from the broad definition of money adopted by Friedman. From this, it follows that the causal relationship between money supply and price level is not settled yet and, therefore, continues to attract the attention of economists (Froyen 2009).

## Demonetization and Quantity Equation

Chanda (2016) has sought to explain the standard version of quantity equation of money and its probable impact on demonetization. In the Indian context, the total value of all final transactions in the economy includes all informal market activities and also the black economy. The effects of demonetization will vary by sector. Transactions take place in the formal sector with both cash and other forms of money. In the short run, this sector might suffer the least. The formal sector transactions also include illegal payments—for example, property transactions and government services. If demonetization works, then in the longer run, the effect would be to reduce the portion of the price that is paid in black money in this sector. The informal sector of the economy which is not illegal but is not correctly recorded in national accounts either. Usually, the government relies on sample surveys to estimate the size of this sector to incorporate into GDP. Depending on the degree of the mismeasurement, this also leads to an underestimate of the true velocity of money in the

Indian economy. One of the claimed benefits of demonetization is that it will also reduce the size of the informal sector (and increase the size of the formal sector). Since demonetization seeks to reduce corruption and if corruption were to actually decline, the portion of the price that is paid in black money in this sector should go down along with diminishing the possibility of the mismeasurement of the informal sector.

# CHAPTER 6

# Demonetization in Other Countries

As a monetary measure, demonetization has been implemented in other countries, too. One can find a series of moves toward demonetization the world over in the past. This chapter seeks to provide an understanding of why various countries embraced demonetization. Many countries implemented demonetization and benefited from the move, whereas some others failed at it. Almost all countries that had done demonetization had some common objectives—to curb inflation, corruption, and black money—and their government decided to demonetize their high-value denomination notes to get rid of these problems. In fact, India's Economic Survey 2015 to 2016 refers to over 20 countries resorting to demonetization with different purposes and different rationale, and with varying results.

## The United States

Demonetization is currently prohibited in the United States, and the Coinage Act of 1965 applies to all U.S. coins and currency regardless of age. In 1969, the United States under President Richard Nixon declared all bills above $100 null and void in the country to curb the existence of black money and restore the country's sheen. The move was highly successful and is claimed to have been the start of development of the American banking system. The $100 bill is the most widely circulated denomination till date and, presently, is the highest value of denomination in production.

## The United Kingdom

The highest denomination banknote in the United Kingdom is £50, which is essentially 50 to 100 times the smallest denomination note of £1. The United Kingdom effected demonetization by withdrawing the £10 note in 1943 and subsequently in 1945 when an Order in Council was passed empowering the Bank of England to withdraw all its notes after giving a month's notice. Again, in 2010, the UK government asked banks to stop handling €500 notes after a report revealed that they were mainly used by criminals.

## Other Countries

In 1982, **Ghana** stopped 50 cedis notes, which made black economy to flourish. It attempted to tackle tax evasion and empty excess liquidity. This made the people of the country support the black market, and they started investing in physical assets, which obviously made the economy weak.

In **Nigeria**, an anticorruption crackdown was conducted by the military government led by Muhammadu Buhari in 1984. The government issued new currency notes with new colors so that old notes would be rendered unusable within a limited time frame. However, the debt-ridden and inflation-hit country did not take the change well, with the result that the country's economy collapsed.

In 1987, when **Myanmar's** military government demonetized around 80 percent value of money to curb black money and corruption. But this led to a political dispute among the members of the government and subsequently to economic disruption, which, in turn, led to mass protests, resulting in deaths of many people. The move backfired and people started hoarding foreign currencies, losing faith in their own currency.

In January 1991, the **Soviet Union**, under the leadership of Mikhail Gorbachev, withdrew 50 and 100 ruble notes in order to eliminate black money and increase the currency value. The notes accounted for a third of the total money in circulation. This demonetization was carried out along with other financial reforms as part of its economic reform, which resulted in a significant increase in food, transport, and utility prices. The move turned counterproductive, leading to a slide in public confidence, which brought down his authority as it did not go well with the citizens. This also influenced subsequent developments, resulting in the August Coup of 1991 and the Belavezha Accords of December 8, 1991, which led to the dissolution of the USSR. An attempt was made in 1998, which led to a successful redenomination of the ruble, where three zeroes were removed from the denomination of the currency. This was followed by another currency switch in 2010, when two more zeroes were removed from the old currency that went off smoothly.

In **Congo**, Dictator Mobutu Sese Seko's administration laid out the back-to-back currency reforms along with a plan to withdraw the obsolescent currency from the system in 1993. The reform was not well received by the public and resulted in increasing economic disruptions. Mobutu was ousted in 1997.

In **Malaysia**, Prime Minister Tun Dr. Mahathir Mohamad undertook a demonetization exercise back in September 1998 during the Asian financial crisis. That year, Bank Negara announced the demonetization of RM500 and RM1000 denominations and its cessation to be legal tender from July 1, 1999. Members of the public would continue to accept RM500 and RM1000 currency notes at full face value only up to June 30, 1999. During this period, members of the public were encouraged to exchange RM500 and RM1000 currency notes for lower denominations or deposit them at any branch of commercial banks or at any finance company within Malaysia. For the holders of RM500 and RM1000 currency notes abroad, appropriate arrangements were made to facilitate the exchange of these currency notes.[1] This provided some experience with decommissioning the 500 and 1,000 ringgit denominations after the 1997 Asian financial crisis.

## The European Union

In the recent past, a very successful currency changeover operation was carried out in Europe, when twelve EU countries introduced their single currency, the Euro, on January 1, 2002. The countries that joined the European Union in the beginning phased out their respective currencies and adopted the Euro in 2002.

I. In order to switch to the Euro, authorities first fixed exchange rates for the varied national currencies into the Euros.

II. When the Euro was introduced, the old national currencies were demonetized.

III.  However, the old currencies remained convertible into Euros for a while so that a smooth transition through demonetization would be ensured.

The creation of a single currency for the European Union over the period 1998 to 2000 was the largest demonetization and currency issue exercise in the history. The adoption of Euro resulted in demonetization across the various nations of European Monetary Union. In the first few days of 2002, participating countries distributed about 8 billion currency notes and 38 billion coins through 218,000 bank branches and post offices and 2.8 million sales outlets. During the same period, authorities also collected a large proportion of the 9 billion national notes and 107 billion national coins. Although the context is entirely different, it shows how much preparation is needed in the case of massive currency changeover. The European Central Bank prepared for almost 3 years, with everyone fully knowing about the changeover on a particular day. Printing new notes and minting new coins had already started in mid-1998.

Front-loading banks with new notes and coins started almost 3 months in advance. By December 31, 2001, banks were already front-loaded with almost two-thirds of the cash needed in the next few weeks. About 96 percent of coins in value terms were already there in the banks. All the ATMs were preloaded with new cassettes and were activated at midnight. Most ATMs were designed to provide maximum €10 and €20 notes, as it was thought that large denominations would create a change shortage during the changeover. Except for a few in Italy, most other ATMs worked as expected. Despite the fact that most Europeans normally used cards, it was expected that during the initial period, people will use more banknotes.

Further, Euro Zone would stop issuing the 500 Euro note after 2018 and will bring in 100 and 200 Euro banknotes. The Western world is currently engaged in the discussion on whether or not cash was an outdated means of payment in the 21st century (providing shelter for the "shadow economy" rather than merely simplifying the everyday means of payment). The design for the new €100 and €200 banknotes has been unveiled, ahead of entering the circulation in May 2019. Both the notes would have new security features, aimed at making them more difficult to counterfeit. The new notes are smaller than the current versions, meaning they will fit better into people's wallets. They are printed on pure cotton fiber paper and, unlike the new Bank of England polymer notes, do not contain any trace of animal products.[2]

Despite all these preparations, many countries still permitted their legacy currency to remain in circulation for almost 2 months. The European example shows how much advance preparation is required if one were looking for the successful and convenient changeover to new currency notes.[3]

## Australia

It became the first country in the world to release polymer (plastic) notes in 1996 in order to stop widespread counterfeiting. Since the purpose was to replace paper with plastic, changing only the material, it did not have any side effects on the economy. In January 2017, the Australian government set up a task force chaired by Michael Andrew to develop a multipronged policy response to combat the black economy, which was also tasked to look into the future of the country's highest denomination banknote of $100 as well as potentially restrict cash transactions over a certain limit in Australia. It submitted its final report to the government in October 2017. The final report contained 80 recommendations, which span the whole economy. Australia, much like India, wanted to clamp down on the shadow economy.

## North Korea and South Korea

Leader Kim Jong-Il brought a sudden change in the country's currency in December 2009, which resulted in chaos in the wake of economic "reform." The North Korean regime decided to lop off two zeroes from the face value of the old currency, known as the won, in order to banish the black market, and gave North Koreans less than a week to exchange all their old currency notes for the new ones. The government announced that it would limit the amount an individual can exchange to just 100,000 won—or less than $40—at black-market exchange rates and any amount above that threshold would, in effect, be worthless. In response to the citizens' immediate and widespread anger, those limits were raised to 150,000 won in cash and 500,000 won in banknotes. The move sought to punish a broad swath of people in the country who had amassed wealth by engaging in black-market trading. Tightening the government control gave a significant blow to the market.

South Korea too demonetized its currency in 2009. However, it had to be withdrawn later.

## Zimbabwe

The country demonetized its currency as its economy collapsed and inflation reached an unprecedented height in 2015. Zimbabwe used to have $100,000,000,000,000 note (a one hundred trillion dollar note). The Zimbabwean economy went for a toss when President Robert Mugabe issued edicts to ban inflation through laughable value notes. After demonetization, the values of trillion dollars dropped to $0.5 dollar and the currency notes were also put up on eBay. The 3-month-long process involved the expunging of the Zimbabwean dollar from the country's financial system and solidifying the U.S. dollar, Botswana pula, and South African rand as the country's legal tender in a bid to stabilize the economy.

## Philippines

In 2015, the country demonetized its banknotes that had been in circulation for 30 years (introduced in 1985). The new notes, which had been in circulation only since 2010, prevented counterfeiting. From January 2017, the old bills have been demonetized and they no longer have any monetary value.

## Pakistan

It phased out all currency notes with old designs to bring in new designs and security features to its currency. In December 2016, Pakistan's senate passed a resolution to phase out its 5,000 rupee notes in an attempt to curtail black money. In value terms, 5,000 rupee bills accounted for

30 percent of the currency in circulation in the country. Pakistan's government plans to implement this demonetization over the next 3 to 5 years, in contrast to India's accelerated approach. Much like India, Pakistan seeks to fight tax evasion and the stashing of illegal wealth.

## The Middle East

June 2016 saw **Saudi Arabia** banning options and derivatives on Riyal's USD peg. **Libya's** central bank started withdrawing old currency in early 2012 in an attempt to restore liquidity after it found that the vast majority of funds were kept outside the banks. In **Iraq**, even when the Iraqi Swiss Dinar ceased to be legal tender in Iraq, it circulated in the northern Kurdish regions. Despite lacking government backing, it had a stable market value for more than a decade. This example is often cited to demonstrate that the value of a currency is not derived purely from its legal status (but this currency would not be a legal tender).

## Venezuela

The South American country, whose inflation rate was to touch 475 percent, announced on December 11, 2016, that it had demonetized the nation's highest currency denomination of 100-bolivar bill in an attempt to fight speculation and currency hoarding. The Nicolás Maduro–led government gave citizens a 72-hour window before withdrawing the currency, which accounted for 77 percent of the nation's cash in circulation. The old notes were to be replaced, at some specified time, with new ones in denominations between 500 and 20,000 bolivars. The government believed that cross-border mafia was buying Venezuelan bolivars and selling them for high profits in Colombia. However, the government was forced to give citizens an extended deadline for the use of the 100 bolivar bill after a serious shortage of currency led to violent protests and looting and the country went into a severe chaos.

Table 6.1 provides a snapshot of some countries that had done demonetization. As shown in the table, one may find several instances when governments across the world failed to implement currency reforms. The move backfired in Ghana. In Nigeria, the goal to fix a debt-ridden and

*Table 6.1  List of countries where demonetization has taken place in chronological order*

| Country | Year | Objective | Results |
|---|---|---|---|
| Germany | 1923 | To control high domestic prices | Inflation fell |
| USA | 1969 | To curb black money | Success |
| Britain | 1971 | To bring uniformity in currency | Success |
| Ghana | 1982 | To control black money | Failed: people turned to foreign currency |
| Nigeria | 1984 | To fix debt-burdened and inflation-ridden economy | Economy collapsed |
| Myanmar | 1987 | To curb black money | Failed: led political dispute and died thousands of people |
| Zaire | 1990 | A plan to withdraw obsolescent currency from the system | Failed |
| Soviet Union | 1991 | Fight against unearned income, smuggling, and corruption | Failed: the economic system of the USSR was ultimately crushed |
| Australia | 1996 | To tackle black money crisis and improve security features on the notes | Success |
| North Korea | 2010 | To lower down the market of black money | Miserably failed |
| Zimbabwe | 2010 | Sliding out from hyperinflation | Failed |
| Pakistan | 2015 | To get rid from black money, counterfeit currency | Messed up |
| Philippines | 2016 | To preserve the integrity of currency | Success |
| Venezuela | 2016 | To curb inflation and cross-border mafia | Failed: forced to take it back after violent protests, looting, chaos, and death |

inflated economy was not achieved. In Myanmar, the first ever student demonstration was held against this move. In the erstwhile Soviet Union, President Gorbachev faced a coup within 8 months in August 1991 as the move was not a success. The Congo Reform Movement in 1993 resulted in increasing economic disruptions and Mobutu was ousted in 1997. Many other cases of demonetization were from those countries that were struggling to come out of serious economic disequilibrium, and there are countries where the public refused to accept the decision, resulting in a big setback to the government. As regards the recent demonetization, the

*Economist* remarked that "anything India does, Venezuela can do worse. In a dramatic effort to curb corruption, India's government cancelled all its high-denomination banknotes without any warning. Since 98 percent of transactions in India are done in cash, commerce seized up. It is a huge mess, but India will after a while print enough replacement notes. And it has a plausible plan to help its many poor people join the cashless digital economy" (December 15, 2016).[4]

More often than not, the governments and leaders from countries around the world who forced demonetization on people failed to see their dreams come to fruition or faced an ouster. In an attempt to crack down upon the wrongdoings of certain sections, the governments also cause inconveniences to those who have hitherto complied with law and order. How well the resentment among these people is tackled show what determines the success of such an exercise. Lahiri (2016) has pointed out that there were instances when countries like Canada and Singapore discontinued printing some high-value notes and asked banks to return such notes to the central bank without calling them illegal tender. In this context, one must make a distinction between the stoppage of printing of high-value notes, as has happened in Canada and Singapore, and the recent demonetization of high-value notes in India. The important point to note is that unlike these countries, in India, though the old high-value notes could be returned to the RBI, these were no longer legal tenders beyond November 8, 2016. Another difference pertains to the printing of new currency notes. There is not only a new ₹ 500 note but also an even higher denomination note than ₹ 1,000, namely, ₹ 2,000, which has been introduced. History tells us that some countries used demonetization as a tool to have an instant result. In sum, it can be said that countries that have gone for demonetization of their currencies have varied experiences and some of them have worrisome results.

## Endnotes

1. Bank Negara Malaysia. September 12, 1998. "Financial Technology Regulatory Sandbox Framework," Press Release. http://www.bnm.gov .my/index.php?ch=en_press&pg=en_press&ac=3005&lang=en, (accessed September 15, 2018).

2. BBC News. 2018. "New 100 and 200 Euro Notes Unveiled." https://www.bbc.com/news/business-45553129, (accessed September 15, 2018).

3. https://thewire.in/economy/europe-currency-changeover-demonetisation, (accessed September 16, 2018).

4. Venezuela's Lunatic Experiment in Demonetization, *The Economist*, December 15, 2016.

# CHAPTER 7

# History of Demonetization in India

Demonetization was perhaps the biggest step in the Indian economic history. As of now, demonetization of currency notes in India has taken place on three occasions: January 1946, January 1978, and November 2016. This chapter is devoted to the discussion on the demonetization of 1946 and 1978. The next chapter will analyze the recent demonetization of November 2016. The advent of the currency dates back to the Indus Valley Civilization. Kingdoms issued royal seals, that is, coins made of gold, silver, and copper, that kept changing with the rulers and the dynasties. The rupee is named after the silver coin, rupiya, first issued by Sultan Sher Shah Suri in the 16th century and later continued by the Mughal Empire. In 1735, Nadir Shah devalued currency, which led to a surge in inflation, withdrawing his decision subsequently (Rastogi 2016). The RBI has the mandate under the RBI Act of 1934 to regulate the issuing of banknotes in India.

## The Concept of Demonetization

Across the globe, the legitimacy of a nation's currency is an outcome of a solemn promise by the head of the issuing authority. Conceptually and technically, therefore, all money is fiat money. It is as good as its promise to pay and is honored either by the country's central bank or by the government, which issues the currency notes. Demonetization is an act of divesting a currency unit of its status as legal tender, in some cases, replacing it with new currency units, which can be characterized as re-monetization, in which forms of payment are restored as legal tender. It is the process where the government declares the currently running currency notes illegal. When there is a change in national currency, the old unit of currency is replaced with a new currency. Demonetization is the act of changing the existing currency to another form. It is important to remember that the confiscation of money is not the objective of the government's demonetization exercise.

## First Demonetization (January 1946)

Successive governments in India carried out demonetization for a variety of reasons. In 1946, the background was World War II, during which businessmen in India made huge fortunes while supplying the Allied war effort and were concealing their profits from the tax department. According to RBI data, ₹ 1,000 and ₹ 10,000 banknotes were in circulation prior to January 1946. After that, the government demonetized ₹ 1,000 and higher denomination banknotes. The preindependence government of India passed the High Denomination Banknotes (Demonetization) Ordinance. The government promulgated two ordinances on Saturday, January 12, 1946, which was declared a bank holiday. The first ordinance asked the banks to furnish information about the currency holdings of various denominations (₹ 100, ₹ 500, ₹ 1,000, and ₹ 10,000). The second was about telling the public that the denomination currency notes of ₹ 1,000 and above were demonetized; the ₹ 100 banknote was spared.

The currency notes of ₹ 1,000 and ₹ 10,000 were removed from circulation, and people were given little time for exchange. As the notes were accounted only to 3 percent of India's population, it did not affect people's normal life to some extent. People were given 10 days for exchange, which meant the first helpline ended on January 23. This was later extended to February 9, when people had to explain why they could not exchange their currency in the first 10 days. Thus, a time limit was fixed for the exchange of demonetized notes by genuine holders at the RBI, or its agencies, on the basis of their declaration. Their declaration and explanations regarding the source of earnings, etc. were investigated carefully. The exchange was not permitted if the explanation of the source of income was not satisfactory. This caused great difficulty to people.

There seems to be some similarity in the reactions from the public, indicating that there is something cyclical about demonetization. The secrecy with which the current government pulled it off has parallels in 1946. "Never was a secret so well kept in Delhi," wrote the *Times of India* (*ToI*) on January 26, 1946. Even the government officials were left with high-value notes to hand in. The *ToI* wrote that only eight officials knew about the plan, including the RBI governor and the finance member of the Viceroy's Council (the equivalent of today's finance minister). In order to be issued on Saturday, January 12, the ordinance had to be flown in a special plane from Delhi to Poona for the viceroy's signatures. It was then flown back. During the discussions with the RBI Governor Chintaman Deshmukh (later to be Jawaharlal Nehru's finance minister), the officers took notes and typed drafts themselves, without the help of any secretary. "The handwritten notes exchanged between these officials were carefully burnt. No carbon copy of the documents was made or kept." Even extra staff wasn't allocated to the RBI's currency department just in case that raised any suspicion (Doctor 2016).

It was generally believed that the black-market operations not only held the general community to ransom but also concealed from tax authorities and so failed to contribute their proper share to the public revenues at the expense of honest citizens. Demonetization is designed to achieve the purpose of bringing such operations within the knowledge of the government and of the taxing authorities in particular, with results of considerable value both to the government and to the general public.[1]

However, it did not also produce impressive results. The ban really did not have much impact, as the currency of such higher denomination was not accessible to the common people. According to the RBI estimates, through this drive, the government collected ₹ 134 crore of the total ₹ 143 crore available in the market; only ₹ 9 crore was not exchanged, or demonetized. This suggests that only 6.25 percent of the currency was destroyed. Thus, the effect of the ordinance fell short of expectations. For a while, after 1946, black money ceased to be a major issue. It turned out to become more like a currency conversion drive as the government couldn't achieve much of profit in the cash-strapped economy at that time (Kamath 2016). The drive to extinguish the holdings of illegally accumulated cash was not successful.

## The Second Demonetization (January 16, 1978)[2]

The story of the second demonetization starts with a telephone call made to Mr. R. Janakiraman, a senior official in the Chief Accountant's Office in the RBI on January 14, 1978. He was said to come to Delhi for an urgent work regarding the exchange control. On reaching Delhi, he was asked to write the demon ordinance within 24 hours. He asked for the previous ordinance as a guidance. All communications with RBI were shut to ward off any speculation. Morarji Desai was the prime minister in the Janata Party government, which demonetized bank notes of ₹ 1,000, ₹ 5,000, and ₹ 10,000. At that time, the union finance minister was H. M. Patel. On January 16, 1978, the ordinance was announced via All India Radio, at 9 a.m. It was through this news bulletin that people came to know the major policy decision. It was also announced that all the banks and treasuries would remain closed the next day, that is, January 17. On the night of Monday, January 16, 1978, the government withdrew from circulation the currency notes of denomination of ₹ 1,000 and above, in a bid to counter black money in the economy. The 1978 ordinance was promulgated, providing that "all high-denomination bank notes shall, notwithstanding anything contained in Section 26 of the Reserve Bank of India Act, 1934, cease to be legal tender." The ordinance was replaced by the High Denomination Banknotes (Demonetization) Act of 1978 on March 30, 1978.

Union Finance Minister H. M. Patel stated in his budget speech on February 28, 1978, that "the demonetization of high-denomination bank notes was a step, primarily aimed at controlling illegal transactions. It is a part of a series of measures which the Government has taken in the public interest and is determined to take against anti-social elements." The banks were directed to immediately prepare statements of all currency notes of ₹ 1,000, ₹ 5,000, and ₹ 10,000 in their possession. Persons holding such notes could exchange them before January 19, 1978, at the designated branches of the RBI and other public sector banks provided they disclosed the source, the time, and the manner of acquisition along with a proper attestation of identity. If for some reason an individual could not apply for exchange of high-denomination notes by January 19, 1978, they could do so by January 24, 1978 (a week's extension) to the RBI, together with a satisfactory explanation of the reasons for not applying within the earlier time limit.

The then RBI governor I. G. Patel was not in favor of this exercise when Finance Minister H. M. Patel informed him about the decision to demonetize the high-denomination currency notes. According to him, "such an exercise seldom produces striking results. Most people who accept illegal gratification, or are otherwise the recipients of black money, do not keep their ill-gotten earnings in the form of currency for long. The idea that the black money or wealth is held in the form of the notes tucked away in suit cases or pillow cases is naïve. And in any case, even those who are caught napping—or waiting—will have the chance to convert the notes through paid agents as some provision has to be made to convert at par the notes tendered in small amounts for which explanations cannot be reasonably sought. But the gesture had to be made, and produced much work and little gain" (Patel 2002, p. 159).[3]

While making a comparison of the two demonetization efforts, one would notice the critical difference that lies in the quantum. The 1946 and 1978 demonetizations effected really high-value notes, which formed a small part of notes in circulation. It is suggested that one can arrive at the estimates by comparing the denomination of the note with the annual per-capita GDP. In 1960, India's per-capita GDP was ₹ 400 (then currency); in 1978, it was ₹ 1722; whereas in 2016, it was ₹ 103,000 (today's currency). Thus in 1960, a ₹ 1,000 note was 2.5× and in 1978 it was 0.5× per-capita GDP, considerably easy to withdraw. In 2016, the ₹ 500 and ₹ 1,000 currency notes represent 85 percent of physical money in circulation. At that time, it was considerably less.

Demonetization in 1978 was better implemented than in 1946. In the January 1978 episode, currency worth ₹ 1.46 billion (1.7 percent of total notes) in circulation was demonetized. Of this, ₹ 1.0 billion (or 68 percent) was tendered back. In 1978, the value of demonetization was very small (only 0.1 percent of GDP). But most holders of high-denomination notes did not turn up at the bank branches to exchange them. They sold them to others who could present them at the bank, with less suspicion. The element of intended surprise and secrecy was also not well maintained and the 1,000-rupee notes were already out of circulation 1 week before the demonetization. Reportedly, the large amounts of high-denomination notes were sent to the Gulf countries, especially to Dubai and Kuwait, a few days before the ordinance was promulgated. In due course, they were presented to the RBI through official channels of the Middle East-based foreign banks that had a connection with such operations. In spite of these limitations, demonetization served some useful, though limited, purpose (Sabhlok 2016). The major benefits claimed are as follows:

1. It brought out into open cash circulating in the illegal informal economy.
2. The step gave an effective blow to the political use of unaccounted money at that time.
3. The declaration made during the exchange of demonetized notes gave the tax officials clue for further investigation.

## Endnotes

1. The Hindu Centre. 2017. "Public Discussion on Demonetisation and Black Money." https://www.thehinducentre.com/multimedia/archive/03153/Background_Note_No_3153982a.pdf, (accessed September 18, 2018).
2. The RBI history. 2005. (Volume 3, 1967–1981) details how things happened.
3. Mostly Economics. 2016. "Digging through India demonetization history—12 Jan 1946 (Saturday) and 16 Jan 1978 (Monday)." https://mostlyeconomics.wordpress.com/2016/11/11/digging-through-india-demonetization-history-12-jan-1946-saturday-and-16-jan-1978-monday (accessed September 18, 2018).

# CHAPTER 8

# Recent Demonetization of Indian Currency

The recent demonetization was perhaps India's boldest policy experiment in over a quarter of a century. It was an unusual and courageous experiment in a country of the size of India. This chapter describes the mechanism of operation of demonetization of November 8, 2016.

## The Background of the Demonetization

Prior to the demonetization, there was an unprecedented rise in the circulation of high-value notes (₹ 500 and ₹ 1,000) from ₹ 1.5 lakh crore in 2004 to about ₹ 15.5 lakh crore in October 2016, their share in the total currency in circulation going up from 34 percent to over 86 percent. According to the RBI, a third of the high-value notes that moved out of the banking system never returned. One can easily infer that this huge unmonitored cash was financing and further fueling the accumulation of black money in the economy (Gurumurthy 2017).

This was manifest in the steep rise in gold, shares, and land prices by almost 10 times during the 6-year period from 2004 to 2010, as compared to the previous 5 years, 1999 to 2004. That asset price rise was not stoked by the matching real growth. It was the other way round. The spurious rise in asset prices generated the mirage of high growth in India like what happened in the United States prior to 2008. The high GDP growth during 2004 to 2010 was just wealth-led growth. "The working capital of black market operations is believed to be held in a large measure in the form of high denomination notes, and Government is aware of the persistent public demand for effective action against these enemies of public welfare."[1] The Direct Tax Inquiry Committee under the chairmanship of K. N. Wanchoo (1971) was appointed "to examine and suggest legal and administrative measures for countering evasion and avoidance of direct taxes," which suggested demonetization as a measure to unearth and counter the spread of black money. It was not even the first time that the aim of ridding the economy of black money was invoked by the government to demonetize the high-value currency notes. The same reason was put forward in 1946 and 1978 while demonetizing the Indian rupee.

## The Third Demonetization of Indian Currency: November 8, 2016

On the evening of November 8, 2016, when Prime Minister Narendra Modi, in a nationally televised broadcast, announced that ₹ 500 and ₹ 1,000 denomination notes would cease to be the legal tender from that midnight, he specified three objectives of such a step: (i) checking counterfeit currencies, (ii) fighting black money, and (iii) countering subversive activities that were harming India's security and economy. The whole country received the announcement with awe and dismay. However, the lower denomination ₹ 10, ₹ 20, ₹ 50, and ₹ 100 notes and the coins were to continue to be valid. He further announced that the new notes of ₹ 500 and ₹ 2,000 would be introduced shortly. On October 28, 2016, the total number of banknotes in circulation in India was 17.77 trillion (U.S. $260 billion). In terms of value, total banknotes in circulation stood at 16.42 trillion (U.S.$240 billion), of which nearly 86 percent (around 14.18 trillion, or U.S.$210 billion) were ₹ 500 and ₹ 1,000 banknotes.[2] They were taken out of circulation from November 8, 2016. The demonetization was announced and took effect with, perhaps, the shortest lag in an economic policy decision of such a high magnitude.

In this context, it would be good to remember that a new ₹ 500 note was introduced in 1987 and ₹ 1,000 was reintroduced in the year 2000 in substantial quantity to contain inflation. The RBI earlier removed pre-2005 notes of all denominations from circulation as they had fewer security features compared to the new notes. The process of removing the older notes from circulation continued for nearly 1 year. The deadline was extended until December 2015, and those notes continued to remain a legal tender until November 8, 2016. This was not exactly demonetization, but removing from circulation, and has now subsumed into the present demonetization. In November 2016, new currency notes of ₹ 500 and ₹ 2,000 were introduced.

## Differences between 1978 and 2016

The following are the distinctive features of demonetizations of 1978 and 2016 (Rajakumar and Shetty 2016):

I. In the January 1978 episode, currency worth ₹ 1.46 billion (1.7 percent of total notes in circulation) was demonetized. Of this, ₹ 1.0 billion (or 68 percent) was tendered back. In 1978, the value of demonetization was very small (only 0.1 percent of GDP). However, the 2016 demonetization effort covers 86 percent of the total currency in circulation (11 percent of GDP).

II. In 1978, ₹ 1,000 and higher value notes were almost impossible to possess in earlier years for the common man given the value of these amounts then. Because of that, demonetization received limited public attention and had little impact on the daily lives of people. High-denomination notes demonetized at that time formed just a minuscule fraction— about 0.6 percent—of the total currency in circulation. Further, the demonetized notes were of significantly high value, having little use for common people. The current situation is different: the demonetized ₹ 500 and ₹ 1,000 notes constitute 86.9 percent of total notes in circulation by value.

III. In 1978, a large portion—45 percent of the high denomination notes in circulation or about 53 percent of the high denomination notes tendered for conversion—were with banks and government treasuries and not with the public. However, in 2016, only ₹ 96,080 crore or just about 5 percent of the total notes in circulation were with banks and government treasuries. In the first week of November 2016, when the current demonetization took place, about 95 percent of such currencies were with the public.

IV. The motivation behind the 1978 and 2016 actions is important. According to the RBI, in recent years, there has been an increased incidence of fake notes in higher denominations, and those notes are used by terrorists and black money hoarders. The annual growth rates in total currency, as well as those in high-denomination notes, have been much higher than the nominal GDP growth (Rajakumar and Shetty 2016).

Here, it is interesting to note that unlike in 2016, in 1978, the government did not have the backing of I. G. Patel, the then RBI governor, who was not in favor of the step. He believed that the ban was implemented simply to immobilize the funds of the opposition party. Patel also believed that people never store black money in the form of currency for too long. It didn't have much effect on the people and affected only the privileged few. He asserted that steps like these rarely have striking results. However, the November 2016 ban had shaken the whole country.

## Legal Aspect of Demonetization in India[3]

Let us now look at some legal aspect of demonetization in India. Like every economic and political measure, demonetization also has a valid place in the Indian law books. The legal basis for demonetizing currency can be found in Section 26 of the Reserve Bank of India Act, 1934. Under subsection (2) of this section, the union government is given the power to declare that any notes issued by the RBI will no longer be legal tender. The only procedural requirement is that the Board of the RBI recommends the same to the union government. In fact, in 1978, demonetization was carried out under a special legislation, namely, the High Denomination Bank Notes (Demonetization) Act, 1978. Former Prime Minister Morarji Desai announced the ban over the radio, after which the banks were closed the following day. In 2016, Narendra Modi announced the currency ban in an address that was broadcasted across all news channels. Both the affairs were kept confidential. The previous demonetization exercises were carried out through ordinance, which later became law passed by the competent legislature. In the present case, the legal tender law was all that was changed in the government's demonetization order.

# Judicial Review

While demonetization *per se* is probably legally sound, a number of legal issues were raised and some 40 petitions are pending disposal before the Supreme Court (SC) and around 50 before various high courts. The SC decided to examine all the aspects of demonetization. It referred to the larger issue of examining the constitutional validity of the decision to a five-judge bench on December 16, 2016. The apex court framed nine issues for adjudication by a five-judge Constitution Bench for authoritative pronouncement on the government's demonetization decision. It also stayed the hearing of all petitions related to demonetization filed in various high courts in the country. The following are the nine queries to be addressed by the SC[4]:

I. Is the notification dated November 8, 2016, *ultra vires* Section 26(2) and Sections 7, 17, 23, 24, 29, and 42 of the Reserve Bank of India Act, 1934?

II. Does the notification contravene the provisions of Article 300(A) of the constitution?

III. Assuming the notification has been validly issued under the RBI Act, 1934, is it *ultra vires* of Articles 14 and 19 of the constitution?

IV. Does the limit on withdrawal of cash from the funds deposited in bank accounts have no basis in law and violates Articles 14, 19, and 21?

V. Does the implementation of the impugned notification(s) suffer from procedural and/or substantive unreasonableness and thereby violates Articles 14 and 19 and, if so, to what effect?

VI. In the event that Section 26(2) is held to permit demonetization, does it suffer from excessive delegation of legislative power, thereby rendering it *ultra vires* of the constitution?

VII. What is the scope of judicial review in matters relating to fiscal and economic policy of the government?

VIII. Whether a petition by a political party on the issues raised is maintainable under Article 32?

IX. Whether district cooperative banks have been discriminated against by excluding them from accepting deposits and exchanging demonetized note?

An important point to note in the SC's interim order is that it recognized that in economic matters it should adopt a "stay off" policy.

## Objectives

Monetary reforms are generally done to deal with conditions of hyperinflation, black money hoarding, and corruption. The demonetization strategy tried before had limited success. The objective of the earlier demonetization was not the same, so comparing them to the current situation would not be proper. It is important to note that the situation in India is completely different from what it was in other countries at the time of demonetization. India is not the only country with rising anticash movement as the fight against cash-dominated economy is to stay and could well intensify (Butani 2016). The present demonetization has many objectives, and the rationale given by the government is as follows:

I. The major objective was to attack the menace of black money/parallel economy/shadow economy.

II. The cash circulation in India is directly connected to corruption; hence, it wants to reduce the cash transactions. India is more reliant on cash as a form of transactions compared to other countries. India has one of the highest levels of currencies in circulation, which is more than 12 percent of its GDP value; the ₹ 1,000 and ₹ 500 notes account for 24.4 percent (around 2,300 crore pieces) of currencies in circulation but for over 85 percent in terms of the value of the currency in circulation.[5] Eliminating high-value notes will shrink the use of black money generation avenues.

III. Demonetization would be a major step toward forming a cashless economy.

IV. It would tackle the threat of counterfeit currency.

V. It would prevent terrorist activities/terror funding as cash is being used for such purposes.

Globally, the biggest sectors that have shadow economies happen to be those that are extremely cash reliant, like construction, real estate, trading, transport, and wholesale and retail businesses. The financial corruption involved the currency notes of bigger denominations, which shatter down the economic, social, as well as political stability of a country. Terrorism and terror funding, human trafficking, drugs, money laundering, counterfeits, and politics, all require anonymity for survival. The objective of ending all these menace is expected to be achieved through demonetization.

Counterfeit money has been an ongoing problem and is often tied to "terror" or insurgency funding. Counterfeit notes, mostly in high denominations—injected into India through porous border with neighboring countries—have been a matter of great concern for quite some time. Pakistan has been printing fake Indian currency at its government printing press in Quetta and its security press in Karachi. The enemy nation funnels the counterfeit currency through the frontier at Jammu and Kashmir and via India's porous border with Bangladesh and Nepal.[6] Besides diluting the underlying strength of the economy, this has been the cheapest source of terror financing in India. Detecting counterfeit notes, chasing culprits responsible for pumping such notes into India, and weeding them out from an economy of this country through enforcement agencies have been a Herculean task.[7] A study conducted by Indian Statistical Institute (ISI), Kolkata, on behalf of the National Investigation Agency (NIA) suggests that fake Indian currency notes (FICN), amounting to ₹ 400 crore, are in circulation in the country at any given point of time and around ₹ 70 crore fake notes are pumped into Indian economy every year. The estimation is based on the recovery and the seizure made by various government agencies. However, the actual figure could be much larger.[8] Most of the fake currencies circulated in India are of ₹ 500 and ₹ 1,000 denominations. In accordance with the global standards, the RBI has now decided to change the security features of higher-denomination banknotes of ₹ 2,000 and ₹ 500, every 3 to 4 years.[9]

The demonetization would cripple the design of financial terrorism by overseas enemies, sometimes operating in connivance with the unscrupulous elements within the country. The root of all these activities is black money. The fungibility of black money reveals that over seven decades, the parallel economy has so spectacularly permeated the life around us that it has got completely intertwined with the formal economy.

Thus, the motivations for demonetization are many. Nayyar (2016) has observed that "a clear separation of the objectives from its consequences would have appealed to a reasoned mind too. The stated objective is economic— to eradicate black money, as also to combat corruption, smuggling, and counterfeit notes. The unstated objective is political. It must be recognized that economics and politics, closely intertwined, are inseparable. Indeed, their interaction is likely to shape future outcomes." Prudent accounting and policy must take note of the larger macroeconomic implications.

Academicians looked at demonetization from different angles—fiscal, monetary, and political. The political motive is to have a sound grasp on the monitoring of defeating tax evasion and corruption ("black money") while increasing oversight of citizen activities. The fiscal and monetary goals are meant to generate higher revenue and force more economic activity into the banking system. It is also expected that demonetization would help in reducing the interest rates in the banking system amid the flush of huge funds and possibility of the passing effect of the fall in the interest rates to the investment in the country (Nataraj 2017). Demonetization has also been considered as a mechanism to drive financial inclusion and use digital financial services (DFS). Demonetization required virtually all adult Indians to engage, directly or indirectly, with a formal financial institution.

In short, the major objectives of the 2016 demonetization of Indian currency were

  I.   To flush out black money,
 II.   To eliminate FICN,
 III.   To strike at the root of financing of terrorism and left-wing extremism,
 IV.   To convert the nonformal economy into a formal one,
  V.   To expand the tax base and employment in the country, and
 VI.   To give a big boost to the digitalization of payments to make India a less-cash economy.

## Operational Mechanism

Demonetization policy has been termed as the greatest financial reform. It is an act of creative destruction. It has become important to everyone because everyone got affected by this—businesspeople, salaried people, housewives, students, working professionals, politicians, etc. The operational mechanics of demonetization were governed by two notifications, issued by India's Ministry of Finance (MoF) and the RBI. Both were issued shortly after the prime minister's announcement. Technically, demonetization meant withdrawing the legal tender character of all existing ₹ 500 and ₹ 1,000 notes and introducing the new notes, valued at ₹ 500 and ₹ 2,000. The two notifications specified how this process was to be regulated, including over-the-counter exchanges of old notes and daily and weekly limits for withdrawals at bank counters and ATMs. The important fact to note is the way demonetization was communicated. There seems to be lack of insight among government bodies about the reasoning behind demonetization.

One issue that dominated the Indian public discourse on demonetization was its evolutionary nature. Between November 8 and December 30, the last day to exchange or deposit old notes, the RBI issued 50 notifications to guide and regulate the process and to remind the actors, namely, public and private sector banks, of their legal obligations. Some of these were of an advisory nature but a large proportion provided substantive changes to the workings of the system. The MoF, for its part, issued 19 notifications during the same time frame, some reflecting RBI notifications and others introducing additional changes. The number of modifications was so large that the RBI created a website entitled "All you wanted to know from RBI," referencing the 57 notifications and 27 press releases (as of March 1, 2017) that the central bank had issued on demonetization (RBI 2017).[10]

From the public's perspective, the most visible changes to the operational mechanics of demonetization concerned exchanging and depositing old notes, as well as caps on the availability of new notes. By the end of the year 2016, the RBI had issued nine notifications on the exchange and deposit process and five on the cash-withdrawal limits. A significant set of the RBI and MoF notifications pertained to the agricultural sector, where nearly half of India's population is employed, addressing complaints that farmers were unable to purchase supplies for the ongoing sowing season. The criticism leveled against demonetization led to a number of modifications to the operational mechanics of demonetization, which, in turn, led to accusations that the government had failed to think through the operation properly (Beyes and Bhattacharya 2017).

These frequent and often sudden operational changes had a direct impact on the population. Policy makers, with their own actions, destabilized a perfectly stable and one of the fastest growing economies in the world. The authorities must have known that changing notes was going to be a huge logistical exercise. It seems that the government is simply trying to learn through the trial-and-error method. Bank employees had worked continuously without taking a day off. Their cooperation matters a lot. Given this scenario, demonetization was resorted to tackle distortions in the economy. The fact is cash economy has moved deep into the Indian economy. But it is important to remember that by and large cash economy does not connote illicit economy. The problem lies in its unorganized economy.

## Endnotes

1. Choudhury, S. 2016. "Demonetisation: Newspaper Headlines from 1946 Tell a Story Similar to 2016." https://www.news18.com/news/india/demonetization-newspaper-headlines-from-1946-tell-a-story-similar-to-2016-1311844.html, (accessed September 20, 2018).
2. The Annual Report of RBI 2015 to 2016.
3. Testbook. 2018. "Important Questions & Facts about Demonetization in India for Bank and SSC." https://testbook.com/blog/important-questions-facts-about-demonetization-banking-ssc, (accessed September 20, 2018).
4. LiveLaw News Network. 2016. "#Demonetisation: Read Nine Questions Referred to Constitution Bench [Read Order]." https://www.livelaw.in/demonetization-read-nine-questions-referred-constitution-bench-read-order, (accessed September 20, 2018).
5. BYJU'S. 2018. "Understanding Demonetization a Critical Analysis." https://byjus.com/free-ias-prep/demonetization-of-rs-500-and-rs-1000, (accessed September 21, 2018).
6. CAclubindia. 2018. "Was Demonetisation Justifiable!" https://www.caclubindia.com/articles/was-demonetization-justifiable—31704.asp, (accessed September 21, 2018).

7. The Hindu Businessline. 2018. "Demonetisation's Good Policy Too." https://www.thehindubusinessline.com/opinion/demonetizations-good-policy-too/article9330233.ece, (accessed September 21, 2018).

8. OpIndia. 2017. "Banks Caught More Fake Currencies in 2015 than Earlier." https://www.opindia.com/2017/06/banks-caught-more-fake-currencies-in-2015-than-earlier, (accessed September 21, 2018).

9. *The Times of India*, April 2, 2017.

10. RBI. 2017. All You wanted to know from RBI about Withdrawal of Legal Tender Status of Rs. 500 and 1000 Notes. https://www.rbi.org.in/scripts/bs_viewcontent.aspx?Id=3270, (accessed September 22, 2018).

# APPENDIX 8.1

Text of the speech by Indian Prime Minister Narendra Modi on Demonetization, November 8, 2016[1]:

My dear citizens,

I hope you ended the festive season of Diwali with joy and new hope. Today, I will be speaking to you about some critical issues and important decisions. Today I want to make a special request to all of you. You may recall the economic situation in May 2014 when you entrusted us with an onerous responsibility. In the context of BRICS, it was being said that the "I" in BRICS was shaky. Since then, we had 2 years of severe drought. Yet, in the last two and a half years with the support of 125 crore Indians, India has become the "bright spot" in the global economy. It is not just we who are saying this; it is being stated by the International Monetary Fund and the World Bank.

In this effort for development, our motto has been "Sab Ka Saath Sab Ka Vikas": We are with all citizens and for development of all citizens. This Government is dedicated to the poor. It will remain dedicated to them. In our fight against poverty, our main thrust has been to empower the poor, and make them active participants in the benefits of economic progress.

The Pradhan Mantri Jan Dhan Yojana, the Jan Suraksha Yojana, the Pradhan Mantri Mudra Yojana for small enterprises, the Stand-up India program for Dalits, Adivasis and women, the Pradhan Mantri Ujjwala Scheme for gas connections in the homes of the poor, the Pradhan Mantri Fasal Beema Yojana and Pradhan Mantri Krishi Sinchai Yojana to protect the income of farmers, the Soil Health Card Scheme to ensure the best possible yield from farmers' fields, and the e-NAM National Market Place scheme to ensure farmers get the right price for their produce—these are all reflections of this approach.

In the past decades, the specter of corruption and black money has grown. It has weakened the effort to remove poverty. On the one hand, we are now no.1 in the rate of economic growth. But on the other hand, we were ranked close to one hundred in the global corruption perceptions ranking 2 years back. In spite of many steps taken, we have only been able to reach a ranking of seventy-six now. Of course, there is improvement. This shows the extent to which corruption and black money have spread their tentacles.

The evil of corruption has been spread by certain sections of society for their selfish interest. They have ignored the poor and cornered benefits. Some people have misused their office for personal gain. On the other hand, honest people have fought against this evil. Crores of common men and women have lived lives of integrity. We hear about poor auto-rickshaw drivers returning gold ornaments left in the vehicles to their rightful owners. We hear about taxi drivers who take pains to locate the owners of cell phones left behind. We hear of vegetable vendors who return excess money given by customers.

There comes a time in the history of a country's development when a need is felt for a strong and decisive step. For years, this country has felt that corruption, black money and terrorism are festering sores, holding us back in the race towards development.

Terrorism is a frightening threat. So many have lost their lives because of it. But have you ever thought about how these terrorists get their money? Enemies from across the border run their operations using fake currency notes. This has been going on for years. Many times, those using fake 500 and 1,000 rupee notes have been caught and many such notes have been seized.

Brothers and sisters,
On the one hand is the problem of terrorism; on the other is the challenge posed by corruption and black money. We began our battle against corruption by setting up an SIT headed by a retired Supreme Court judge, immediately upon taking office. Since then a law was passed in 2015 for disclosure of foreign black money;

- agreements with many countries, including the USA, have been made to add provisions for sharing banking information;
- a strict law has come into force from August 2016 to curb be- nami transactions, which are used to deploy black money earned through corruption;
- a scheme was introduced for declaring black money after paying a stiff penalty; My dear countrymen,

Through all these efforts, in the last two and a half years, we have brought into the open nearly 1 lakh 25 thousand crore rupees of black money belonging to the corrupt. Honest citizens want this fight against corruption, black money, benami property, terrorism and counterfeiting to continue. Which honest citizen would not be pained by reports of crores worth of currency notes stashed under the beds of government officers? Or by reports of cash found in gunny bags?

The magnitude of cash in circulation is directly linked to the level of corruption. Inflation becomes worse through the deployment of cash earned in corrupt ways. The poor have to bear the brunt of this. It has a direct effect on the purchasing power of the poor and the middle class. You may yourself have experienced when buying land or a house, that apart from the amount paid by check, a large amount is demanded in cash. This creates problems for an honest person in buying property. The misuse of cash has led to artificial increase in the cost of goods and services like houses, land, higher education, health care and so on. High circulation of cash also strengthens the hawala trade which is directly connected to black money and illegal trade in weapons. Debate on the role of black money in elections has been going on for years.

Brothers and sisters,

To break the grip of corruption and black money, we have decided that the ₹ 500 and ₹ 1,000 currency notes presently in use will no longer be legal tender from midnight tonight that is November 8, 2016. This means that these notes will not be acceptable for transactions from midnight onwards. The ₹ 500 and ₹ 1,000 notes hoarded by antinational and anti-social elements will become just worthless pieces of paper. The rights and the interests of honest, hard-working people will be fully protected. Let me assure you that notes of ₹ 100, ₹ 50, ₹ 20, ₹ 10, ₹ 5, ₹ 2 and ₹ 1 rupee and all coins will remain legal tender and will not be affected. This step will strengthen the hands of the common man in the fight against corruption, black money and fake currency. To minimize the difficulties of citizens in the coming days, several steps are being taken.

1. Persons holding old notes of ₹ 500 or ₹ 1,000 rupees can deposit these notes in their bank or post office accounts from November 10 till close of banking hours on December 30, 2016 without any limit.

2. Thus you will have 50 days to deposit your notes and there is no need for panic.

3. Your money will remain yours. You need have no worry on this point.

4. After depositing your money in your account, you can draw it when you need it.

5. Keeping in mind the supply of new notes, in the first few days, there will be a limit of ₹ 10,000 per day and ₹ 20,000 per week. This limit will be increased in the coming days.

6. Apart from depositing your notes in your bank account, another facility will also be there.

7. For your immediate needs, you can go to any bank, head post office or sub post office, show your identity proof like Aadhaar card, voter card, ration card, passport, PAN card or other approved proofs, and exchange your old ₹ 500 or ₹ 1,000 notes for new notes.

8. From November 10 till November 24 the limit for such exchange will be ₹ 4,000. From November 25 till December 30, the limit will be increased.

9. There may be some who, for some reason, are not able to deposit their old ₹ 500 or ₹ 1,000 notes by December 30, 2016.

10. They can go to specified offices of the Reserve Bank of India up to March 31, 2017 and deposit the notes after submitting a declaration form.

11. On November 9 and in some places on November 10 also, ATMs will not work. In the first few days, there will be a limit of ₹ 2,000 per day per card.

12. This will be raised to ₹ 4,000 later.

13. ₹ 500 and ₹ 1,000 notes will not be legal tender from midnight. However for humanitarian reasons, to reduce hardship to citizens, some special arrangements have been made for the first 72 hours, that is till midnight on November 11.

14. During this period, government hospitals will continue to accept ₹ 500 and ₹ 1,000 notes for payment.

15. This is for the benefit of those families whose members may be unwell.

16. Pharmacies in government hospitals will also accept these notes for buying medicines with doctors' prescription.

17. For 72 hours, till midnight on November 11, railway ticket book-ing counters, ticket counters of government buses and airline ticket counters at airports will accept the old notes for purchase of tickets. This is for the benefit of those who may be travelling at this time.

18. For 72 hours, ₹ 500 and ₹ 1,000 notes will be accepted also at

    • Petrol, diesel and CNG gas stations authorized by public sector oil companies

    • Consumer co-operative stores authorized by State or Central Government

    • Milk booths authorized by State governments

    • Crematoria and burial grounds.

    These outlets will have to keep proper records of stock and collections.

19. Arrangements will be made at international airports for arriving and departing passengers who have ₹ 500 or ₹ 1,000 rupee notes of not more than 5,000 to exchange them for new notes or other legal tender.

20. Foreign tourists will be able to exchange foreign currency or old notes of not more than ₹ 5,000 into legal tender.

21. One more thing I would like to mention, I want to stress that in this entire exercise, there is no restriction of any kind on noncash pay-ments by checks, demand drafts, debit or credit cards and electronic fund transfer.

Brothers and sisters,

In spite of all these efforts there may be temporary hardships to be faced by honest citizens. Experience tells us that ordinary citizens are always ready to make sacrifices and face difficulties for the benefit of the nation. I see that spirit when a poor widow gives up her LPG subsidy, when a retired school teacher contributes his pension to the Swacch Bharat mission, when a poor Adivasi mother sells her goats to build a toilet, when a soldier contributes ₹ 57,000 to make his village clean. I have seen that the ordinary citizen has the determination to do anything, if it will lead to the country's progress. So, in this fight against corruption, black money, fake notes and terrorism, in this movement for purifying our country, will our people not put up with difficulties for some days? I have full confidence that every citizen will stand up and participate in this "mahayagna." My dear countrymen, after the festivity of Diwali, now join the nation and extend your hand in this *Imandaari ka Utsav*, this *Pramanikta ka Parv*, this celebration of integrity, this festival of credibility.

I am sure that all political parties, all governments, social services organizations, the media and indeed all sections of the society will take part in this with enthusiasm and make it a success.

My dear countrymen,

Secrecy was essential for this action. It is only now, as I speak to you, that various agencies like banks, post offices, railways, hospitals and others are being informed. The Reserve Bank, banks and post offices have to make many arrangements at very short notice. Obviously, time will be needed. Therefore all banks will be closed to the public on November 9. This may cause some hardship to you. I have full faith that banks and post offices will successfully carry out this great task of national importance. However, I appeal to all of you to help the banks and post offices to meet this challenge with poise and determination.

My dear citizens,

From time to time, based on currency needs, the Reserve Bank with the approval of the Central Government brings out new notes of higher value. In 2014, the Reserve Bank sent a recommendation for issue of ₹ 5,000 and ₹ 10,000 notes. After careful consideration, this was not accepted. Now as part of this exercise, RBI's recommendation to issue ₹ 2,000 notes has been accepted. New notes of ₹ 500 and ₹ 2,000 with completely new design will be introduced. Based on past experience, the Reserve Bank will hereafter make arrangements to limit the share of high denomination notes in the total currency in circulation. In a country's history, there come moments when every person feels he too should be part of that moment, that he too should make his contribution to the country's progress. Such moments come but rarely. Now, we again have an opportunity where every citizen can join this mahayajna against the ills of corruption, black money and fake notes. The more help you give in this campaign, the more successful it will be.

It has been a matter of concern for all of us that corruption and black money tend to be accepted as part of life. This type of thinking has afflicted our politics, our administration and our society like an infestation of termites. None of our public institutions is free from these termites.

Time and again, I have seen that when the average citizen has to choose between accepting dishonesty and bearing inconvenience, they always choose to put up with inconvenience. They will not support dishonesty.

Once again, let me invite you to make your contribution to this grand sacrifice for cleansing our country, just as you cleaned up your surroundings during Diwali.

Let us ignore the temporary hardship.

Let us join this festival of integrity and credibility.

Let us enable coming generations to live their lives with dignity.

Let us fight corruption and black money.

Let us ensure that the nation's wealth benefits the poor.

Let us enable law-abiding citizens to get their due share.

I am confident in the 125 crore people of India and I am sure country will get success.

Thank you very much. Thanks a lot.

*Namaskar.*

*Bharat Mata Ki Jai.*

# Endnotes

1. Press Information Bureau, Government of India, Prime Minister's Office, New Delhi. November 8, 2016. http://pib.nic.in/newsite/PrintRelease.aspx?relid=153404, (accessed September 23, 2018).

# CHAPTER 9

# Demonetization in India: A Critique

The 2016 demonetization has divided the citizens of India into two groups, one in its favor and other against it. Desperate times lead to desperate measures. Demonetization gave a new direction to the way people do monetary transactions in India and attempted to destroy the "parallel economy." The big painful jolt of demonetization would create the right psychological milieu for the war against black money. As a cleaning exercise, demonetization can give birth to several good things in the economy. We bring out the major positive and negative consequences of demonetization in the following paragraphs.

## Gains from Demonetization

I. Demonetization is expected to cleanse the formal economic system and throw out the black money. There has been a distinct and positive change in people's attitude against black money. This will do away with the mentality that deals with black money.

II. Most of the businesspeople who have been hiding some income paid advance tax as their current year's income.

III. Individuals are required to submit Permanent Account Number (PAN), allocated by the Income Tax Department of the Government of India, for any deposit above ₹ 50,000 in cash, which will help tax department to track individuals with high denominations.

IV. There has been an increase in the country's tax base. A message has gone out that there's no point any longer in hiding income and the law is now going to come after them.

V. Municipal authorities and revenue departments were getting a very high amount of old dues recovered.

VI. Providing another opportunity to black money holders to legalize their wealth, the government proposed to tax 50 percent of the unaccounted demonetized cash that was disclosed voluntarily until December 30, 2016, after which it was steeped up to 85 percent tax plus penalty levied on undisclosed wealth that would be discovered by the authorities. It also provided for immunity from being questioned on the source of funds.

VII. The have-nots appear to have endorsed the government's decision. The cash hoarded by their immediate employers and exploiters is the most familiar imagery of black money for them. Hence, when that dodgy cash is destroyed, they feel empowered. That is why they are cheering demonetization, although they stand to benefit little from it.

VIII. Importantly, the surge in bank deposits has ended the anonymity of high-value accounts.

IX. There has been a continuous increase in digital payments, resulting in a more formal digital economy.

X. Due to digitalization, the economy could be more transparent. Online payments may clear the business transaction in a more transparent manner.

XI. It would increase the revenue of the government.

XII. Demonetization has helped bring a significant amount of additional money into the formal banking system, which is apparent from the increased number of bank deposits. Nearly 30 crore bank accounts were opened and brought huge savings into the banking system.

XIII. Demonetization has adversely affected multiple militant groups. Left-wing extremists (LWEs) have received a setback because of this. For LWEs, the demonetization move was an "undeclared financial emergency."

XIV. In the short term, the circulation of fake currency has slowed down considerably.

XV. Awareness and conscience can reduce the transaction with black money if follow up measures are taken by the government.

However, a deeper study is required to check the effectiveness of demonetization.

## Critiques of Demonetization

The critics have an altogether different opinion about demonetization. Criticizing demonetization, Paul Krugman said it is "highly disruptive" and will not change the behavior of people, who would become more careful and sophisticated in money laundering. He, however, observed that it is an unusual step, and there is a good case for demonetization of high-value notes.[1] Former prime minister Dr. Manmohan Singh expressed concern over the demonetization policy and said that "waging a war on black money may sound enticing."[2] Targeting black money through demonetization of high-currency notes is recommended by Kenneth Rogoff. A substantial chunk of America's illicit economy is conducted, and its assets parked, in $100 bills. He asserted that demonetization would have a similar impact in India, although long-term gains would be offset by the reintroduction of new high-denomination notes. High-value currency notes are, therefore, mostly used in black economy flows, the profits from which are ultimately converted into black money (Rogoff 2016). Many economists are of the view that the ₹ 2,000 currency note will be much easier to hide and can be used to store black money in lesser space.

Some economists (Bhagwati, Dehejia, and Krishna 2016) observed that demonetization would permanently change the psyche of the tax evader. Others felt that it would lead to more sophisticated forms of tax evasion and black-money hoarding.[3] Demonetization threat must be kept alive, making hoarding not just illegal but unprofitable.[4] Strict oversight of transactions in the areas of the economy where they thrive can alone achieve this result.

Notwithstanding, demonetization has made the situation chaotic. The sudden announcement and severe cash shortages have had a detrimental impact on business and economy. People trying to exchange their banknotes had to stand in long queues, causing many deaths due to inconvenience and rush. Due to the cash crunch, the farmers, especially small and marginal, remained worst affected and could not complete their agricultural activity. The real estate sector came to a standstill and is still gasping for buyers of the constructed and half-constructed buildings. This has resulted in poor cash flow leading to poor demand.

Tempers ran high among the masses as there was a delay in the circulation of new currency. Due to the inability to pay cash to daily wage workers, small employers faced several ordeals to conduct their business activity.[5] The poor planning on the part of the government also added to the woes of the common people with low incomes. There were massive operational challenges.

Looking from the political angle, the entire opposition has stood against demonetization. Former prime minister Dr. Manmohan Singh, along with many economists like Amartya Sen, Kaushik Basu, and Arun Shourie, have criticized demonetization because millions of innocent people were deprived of their money and suffered to get their money back. The move hurt innocent people who had no illegal money but had built up cash reserve over a long period of time. There has been a negative impact in retail trade in goods and services. Currency for everyday transaction was not replaced soon. The scheme had a big loophole. The *Harvard Business Review* reiterated that the policy "was poorly thought out and executed and that its net impact would be negative and particularly bad for the poor."[6]

Compounding the existing confusion about the time frame during which old notes could be exchanged or deposited was the fact that the RBI introduced separate rules for District Central Cooperative Banks (DCCBs) and Primary Agricultural Credit Societies (PACS), the primary financial institutions used by the rural population. From November 14, 2016, onward, DCCBs and PACS were allowed to only issue new currency but not to exchange or credit old notes (Beyes and Bhattacharya 2017).

### Ordeals Faced by the People

I. The initial days after the announcement were *chaotic*. The poor were shocked by the move. Laborers in the textile, footwear, plastic, and metal industry were adversely affected. Laborers in the organized and unorganized sectors bore the brunt of this move. Laborers were compelled to leave from their workplace as they were not paid their wages.

II. Many poor daily wage workers were left with no job and income as owners were unable to pay their daily wage. Chaos over the note ban continued.

III. In the weeks and months after November 8, 2016, Indians cutting across all lines—rich and poor, urban and rural—formed serpentine queues to deposit money and get hold of some precious but rationed cash for much-needed daily use. The police had to be involved to maintain queues at ATMs/banks to withdraw money. On occasions, the police had to resort to *lathi charge* on unruly queues.

IV. Demonetization created some problems for certain types of transactions, such as transportation and daily food expenses.

V. Complex money-laundering networks sprang up in the wake of the demonetization to help wealthy people to deposit huge volumes of previously undeclared currency without exposing themselves to tax authorities. Such people allegedly sold the old notes, at a discount, to brokers, who then dispatched low-income people to deposit or exchange them at banks. Many wealthy people turned to friends and relatives to help them funnel previously undeclared cash into the banking system, while others paid advance salaries to large numbers of workers.

VI. Reduction in illegal activity is expected as the cash provided for such activities has no value now. Corrupt officers and money launderers are under threat as the Income Tax Department is taking all the measures to track such people.

VII. Even in the "Jan Dhan" accounts, as the demonetization experience suggested, there are ample cases of misuse. A total of ₹ 9,800 crore was allegedly credited in the account of a taxi driver in Barnala.[7]

VIII. The government has to bear the cost of printing new currency and its circulation. The cost of printing currency can be viewed as front-loading of retirement of notes.

IX. The chaos and the misstep of the policy could hardly shroud the barren balance sheet of retrieval of black money.

Rogoff (2016) has observed that the long-run gains of demonetization depend on implementation—not intentions, not aspirations, but whether the government can deliver on its promises. The key challenge for the economy is uncertainty. The effect of this policy is not going to be uniform across the economy. The success of the demonetization exercise with respect to the goals (corruption, black money, and mindset shift) other than terrorism should be measured in the following ways (Rajwade 2016):

A) Above-trend increase in the number of income-tax filers and payers, in the ratio of non-corporate income tax to GDP;
B) Reduction in employment in the informal sector and rise in employment in the formal sector;
C) An increase in the average size of factories and production units in terms of employment and output.

The issue of demonetization may be looked at from multiple perspectives. It is important to note that the demonetization drive has earned Modi kudos from the global media. In a glowing tribute, the Singapore-based newspaper the *Independent* stated: "Modi does a Lee Kuan Yew to stamp out corruption in India." The paper compared him to late Lee Kuan Yew, the nation-state's founding father. Forbes also patted him saying "despite chaos, it is working." The *New York Times*, quoting analysts, also endorsed it as "a wise move." Even China's *Global Times* described the move as "startling and bold." However, it is good to reform by all means but with a human face.[8]

# Endnotes

1. Note Ban "Highly Disruptive": Nobel Laureate Krugman, *The Tribune*, December 2016.
2. Indian National Congress. 2018. "The Year 2018 when India Resisted." https://www.inc.in/en/in-focus/making-of-a-mammoth-tragedy, (accessed September 24, 2018).
3. Mangla, A. 2017. "Demonetization: The Politics of Visible Disruption." https://casi.sas.upenn.edu/iit/amangla, (accessed September 24, 2018).
4. Desai, M. 2016. "Modi has by Fiat Made Hoards of Cash Valueless," *MINT*, November 13, 2016.

5. MBA Universe. 2018. "Demonetization: Success & Failures." https://www.mbauniverse.com/group-discussion/topic/business-economy/demonetisation, (accessed February 21, 2019).

6. https://indianexpress.com/article/business/business-others/harvard-business-review-lists-out-four-lessons-for-the-world-to-learn-from-indias-demonetisation-move-4920309, (accessed February 21, 2019).

7. Goyal, B. B. 2016. "Punjab: How a Taxi Driver Got ₹ 9,806 crore in his Jan Dhan account," *News Headline, Hindustan Times*, November 29, 2016.

8. Demonetization: Modi's "India Shining" Moment? *The Free Press Journal*, November 18, 2016.

# APPENDIX 9.1

## List of the Rules Set

Before the prime minister issued an order to demonetize certain currency, he consulted the RBI and the finance minister. Here is a list of the rules set in place continuously over a time of 20 days since the prime minister announced demonetization during the month of November 2016:

| Date | Events |
|---|---|
| November 8 | PM declares the ₹ 500 & ₹ 1,000 notes invalid/illegal. Exchange of cash up to ₹ 4,000 allowed at banks, ATM withdrawal limited to ₹ 2,000. |
| November 9 | Banks remain shut for a day. |
| November 10 | Banks open. Massive queues ensue as millions line up to exchange old currency or deposit their money. |
| November 12 | Reports come in that people died waiting in the queues. The Sensex registers the biggest single-day fall in 9 months. |
| November 13 | ATM withdrawal limit raised to ₹ 2,500; cash exchange limit raised to ₹ 4,500. |
| November 15 | Banks are asked to apply indelible ink marks on people exchanging money. The Election Commission raises concerns regarding this advice. |
| November 16 | Parliament session begins; the opposition parties raise their voice against the government over the sufferings of the poor. |
| November 17 | Currency exchange limit lowered to ₹ 2,000. |
| November 18 | India's Supreme Court says many are "frantic" over demonetization. |
| November 22 | RBI says banks have received ₹ 5.3 lakh crore in deposits since November 8. |
| November 24 | The government orders that old notes can now only be deposited at banks and not exchanged. |
| November 27 | Former RBI governor Urjit Patel justifies demonetization, says the new notes are difficult to counterfeit. |

# APPENDIX 9.2

## Operational Problems

### Cash Crunch across the Country

There was a considerable amount of cash crunch in the entire nation. Soon after the scheme was announced, there were long and serpentine queues outside banks and ATMs. Even after 1 month, people continued to deal with the cash crunch. Queues outside banks continued even as banks across public and private sectors complained of not having enough cash to meet the people's needs.

### RBI's Guidelines for Cash Withdrawal

The government and the RBI changed rules for withdrawal, exchange, and deposit of cash several times since demonetization. In days that followed the rollout of new currency notes on November 10, the use of old notes was completely scrapped out, and then the deadline was extended for petrol pumps, tolls, and government medical stores. ATM withdrawal limits were repeatedly changed from ₹ 4,000 to ₹ 2,500 to ₹ 2,000.

### Timeline

Here is a timeline of how the days passed:

> **November 9:** Banks and ATMs remained closed for the public on the first day of demonetization.
> - Any amount deposited above 2.5 lakhs faced tax.
> - Government suspended highway toll till November 11.
> **November 10:** Banks across India witnessed long queues to exchange and deposit annulled notes witnessed at banks across India, while the ATMs remained shut.
> **November 11 to 12:** ATMs opened for the first time after demonetization announcement. But, after opening, most ATMs went dry in

a few hours with people drawing the maximum possible amount; long queues were seen across the country, in selected places like government hospitals and petrol pumps.

○ Toll waiver on national highways extended until the midnight of November 14 by the government.

**November 13:** Currency exchange limit increased from ₹ 4,000 to ₹ 4,500.

○ ATM withdrawal limit increased from ₹ 2,000 to ₹ 2,500.

○ The weekly limit of ₹ 20,000 for withdrawal from bank counters was increased to ₹ 24,000. The maximum limit of ₹ 10,000 per day on such withdrawals was removed.

**November 14:** Government extended acceptance of ₹ 500 and ₹ 1,000 notes for public utility and fuel payment till November 24.

○ Cash withdrawal for current account holders increased to ₹ 50,000 per week.

○ Charges on ATM transactions waived till December 30.

**November 15 to 16:** No relief from long queues at banks and ATMs.

○ Government asked banks to put indelible ink on the right-hand finger of those exchanging banned 500 and 1,000 rupee notes.

○ SBI collected ₹ 1,14,139-crore in deposits in 7 days.

**November 17:** Government lowered the exchange limit for now-defunct 500 and 1,000 rupee notes to ₹ 2,000 from the existing cap of ₹ 4,500

○ Cash withdrawal of ₹ 2.5 lakh from bank account was allowed for wedding ceremonies.

○ Government eased cash withdrawal limit for farmers by allowing them to withdraw up to ₹ 50,000 cash per week from bank.

○ Government extended toll exemption on national highways until November 24 midnight.

**November 18 to 20:** No respite from queues, chaos; ATMs continued to fight cash shortage.

○ Congress party alleged that 55 people had died due to demonetization; sought the prime minister's apology.

○ Queues got shorter at banks; long wait at ATMs continued.

**November 21:** Farmers allowed to use old ₹ 500 notes for buying seeds.

- Bank received ₹ 5.12 lakh crore of deposits and exchanged ₹ 33,006 crore, RBI said in a release.

**November 22:** 82,500 ATMs out of 2.2 lakh ATMs recalibrated to dispense new notes.

- Some relief for cash-starved public, queues shortened as about 40 percent of total ATMs started dispensing new ₹ 500 and ₹ 2,000 notes.

**November 24:** Government extended toll exemption on national highways until December 2, midnight.

- Government withdrew exchange facility of old currency notes and extended the deadline for exemptions from using old ₹ 500 notes up to December 15 midnight.

**November 25:** RBI said the facility to exchange old ₹ 500 and ₹ 1,000 notes would continue to be available at its counters.

- Queues at banks thin, but some branches still faced cash pain.

**November 26 to 30:** Deposits in *Jan Dhan* accounts rose sharply by around ₹ 27,200 crore to ₹ 72,834.72 crore in just 14 days after the announcement of the ban on old ₹ 500 and ₹ 1,000 currency notes.

- ₹ 32,631 crore deposited in post offices since demonetization.
- Banks got about ₹ 8.45 lakh crore worth of scrapped notes, as per the RBI.

**December 1 to 3:** Government said that old ₹ 500 notes would be valid until December 2, for fuel and air ticket purchase instead of the earlier announced date of December 15.

9. 80 lakh ATMs were recalibrated to dispense ₹ 500 and ₹ 2,000 notes.

**December 6 to 7:** Tax department seized ₹ 130 crore cash, jewelry, and ₹ 2,000 crore of undisclosed wealth admitted by taxpayers post demonetization.

By January 15, 2017, the limit of cash withdrawal from banks was increased. Also, there was a huge announcement on January 30 from the Prime Minister's Office that from February 1, 2017, there would be no limit on any withdrawals done from the ATMs. The common people heaved a sigh of relief after this.

The limited-period window for exchange of junked ₹ 500 and ₹ 1,000 notes by Indians residing abroad ended on March 31, 2017, with many failing to do so because of limited counters and lack of procedural awareness. However, additional time period of 3 months was made available to nonresident Indians (NRIs) with a rider of exchange of ₹ 25,000 per individual. The exchange window for NRIs closed on June 30. NRIs coming to India were required to do so through Red Channel, disclosing to the customs authorities at the airport the amount of now-defunct notes and secure a certificate to be tendered at the RBI at the time of exchange. The promulgation of the Specified Bank Notes (Cessation of Liabilities Ordinance) Ordinance, December 30, 2016, imposes penal liabilities on the holders of scrapped notes after the specified date. It makes holding, transfer, and receiving of the demonetized notes a criminal offense, punishable with a fine of ₹ 10,000 or five times the cash held, whichever is higher.

As the days passed by, the long queues in ATMs drained away and the cash crunch became history. After these forgetful days, the whole demonetization buzz calmed down in the month of December. However, it did make a difference for moving on to cashless transaction where most of the small outlet or shops in the metro cities as well as in the rural areas started using *Paytm and Freecharge* applications for their transactions. This policy of the government passed off peacefully because of us, the people. By the end of March 2017, after around 5 months of the announcement, the condition had improved significantly and became near normal.

# CHAPTER 10

# Impact on Indian Economy

Like a carpet bombing, demonetization impacts everyone. It could be termed as the mother of all reforms. The move has far-reaching implications. Demonetization technically is a liquidity shock; a sudden stop in terms of currency availability. Such a disruptive policy must have a significant impact on the economy. It creates a situation where the lack of currency jams consumption, investment, production, and employment. The exercise may have short-term as well as long-term impact on consumption, investment, welfare, and growth of the economy. The intensity of the effects of demonetization depends on the duration of the liquidity shocks. The change has got quick pain with a promise of long-term gain, but we have to remember that a large section of our society will need quick gains to survive before they can enjoy the long-term benefits. The impact of demonetization on Indian economy can be discussed under following headings:

    I.  GDP and economic growth
   II.  Agriculture and allied sectors
  III.  Informal sector and micro, small, and medium enterprises (MSMEs)
  IV.  Real estate
   V.  Labor and employment
  VI.  Digital transaction systems
 VII.  Financial sector
VIII.  Government revenues
  IX.  Political parties
   X.  Other economic entities

Some of the impacts will have a lasting effect on the economy in the long run. The aspects of corruption and black money are so important that they are discussed in the next chapter.

# GDP and Economic Growth

Demonetization served as a negative shock to the economy. The GDP formation got impacted by this measure, with a reduction in the consumption and investment demand because:

Consumption $\downarrow \rightarrow$ Production $\downarrow \rightarrow$ Employment $\downarrow \rightarrow$ Growth $\downarrow$. Reduced consumption, income, investment, etc. reduced India's GDP growth. The January to March 2017 quarter was scanned with a critical eye to know what impact demonetization had on the economy. The overall growth rate of GDP was 6.1 percent, which is nearly 1 percent below the growth rate for the previous quarter at 7 percent. It is difficult to decipher how much of the decline in growth rate was due to demonetization and how much due to the underlying declining trend. As rightly observed by C. Rangarajan (2017), while analyzing the January to March quarter numbers, one needs to keep in mind three factors:

I. A decline in the growth rate was observed from the beginning of the year. The growth rate of every quarter was sliding from the previous quarter.

II. During Quarter 4, the only two sectors that had shown strong growth were agriculture and public administration.

III. The sectors that had shown a sharp decline were construction, trade, hotels, transport, and communication.

All these comprise a significant number of informal sector enterprises and provide substantial employment. The growth momentum built up in the earlier months was derailed by demonetization. These are the sectors that use cash extensively. However, the decline in construction should be interpreted carefully. Obviously, the liquidity crunch brought about by inadequate availability of currency as a consequence of demonetization must have halted a lot of construction activity immediately. But the decline was also partly due to "shock effect." After all, the construction and real-estate sectors are notorious for their cash transactions and dealings, which are not above board. There is a paramount need for the participants to adjust.

A question was raised whether demonetization had adversely affected the GDP growth. The answer to this will remain inconclusive until the time when some research can isolate the impact of demonetization from other factors, which include slowing global trade. While the overall GDP growth may have now adjusted to the shock of demonetization, new evidence from the World Bank highlights the scale of its local impact in the months after November 2016. The study used unconventional tools to assess the impact of demonetization. It used the intensity of lights in evenings and at nights to gauge economic activities.

The study conducted by Robert Beyer and others on the South Asia office of the World Bank used this tool to assess three disruptions in South Asia: earthquakes in Nepal, conflict zones in Afghanistan, and demonetization in India. Evening and nighttime lights serve as a good proxy for economic activity and, consequently, economic growth, as consumption and production during that time require some form of lighting. There was a dip in nightlight intensity during the time of demonetization, but it lasted only for about 2 months. This showed that demonetization had a small and short-lived effect on the economic activity in India at the aggregate level. However, the local impact might have been large in more informal-activity districts, where cash must have played a more important role in supporting transactions (Beyer et al. 2018). The conclusion of the study is very natural because demonetization's impact was greatest in rural districts with lower banking access and more informal workers.

## Impact on Agriculture and Allied Sectors

Demonetization has affected every Indian, but it has hit the agricultural sector to the core. India's 263 million farmers live mostly in the cash economy. Agricultural associations complained that farmers across India were unable to sell recently harvested summer crops or purchase seeds for the upcoming winter sowing season. Farmers, in particular, depend on the District Central Cooperative Banks (DCCBs) and Primary Agricultural Credit Societies (PACS) heavily, including when it comes to purchasing seeds and fertilizers. Although the RBI did not present any official reasons for putting restrictions in place, it was speculated that the government was concerned with what was perceived to be unusually large cash deposits at DCCBs and PACS immediately after the demonetization announcement. Between November 8 and 14, DCCBs in 17

Indian states received deposits of approximately 90 billion rupees. The RBI implicitly questioned the source of wealth of depositors' of marginal agriculturists whose overall transactions were not of high volume in the marginal agriculture sector, reportedly raising concerns that DCCBs were used to park unaccounted funds and launder unaccounted income (Fernandes and Sukhi 2016).

The timing of this decision coincided with the peak agricultural season of harvesting summer crops and sowing winter crops. This disrupted cultivation adversely affected the marketing and sale of agricultural produce as traders were unable to pay in cash. The difficulties of the producers of perishables were particularly acute. Further, the input side was equally affected as many payments/purchases, such as for seeds, fertilizers, implements, and tools, or to agricultural workers for farm operations, were outright in cash. The withdrawal of the old currency notes had put pressure on the *mandis*; farmers were having problems in selling their produce as both the parties had to agree on the mode of payment. It was really a tough time for the farmers, who were unable to sell their crop after harvest, as the *mandi*/APMC was unable to make payment to farmers due to cash crunch. Thus, the prices crashed and the wages fell. The agricultural sector experienced volatility in pricing shortly after demonetization, and opposing claims have been made whether prices rose or fell in the aftermath of demonetization. It is possible that price fluctuation was due to seasonalities.

Agriculture was badly hit, and this had a knock-on effect on the non-agricultural unorganized sector, which, in turn, impacted the organized sector. Sale, transport, marketing, and distribution of ready produce to wholesale centers or *mandis* were dominantly cash dependent. Disruptions broke in the supply chain feedback to farmers as sales fell, wastage of perishables increased, lower revenues showed up as trade dues instead of cash in hand, and revenues credited into bank accounts with limited access affected the sector (Kohli 2016).

Simultaneously, many of these networks were operating sub-optimally depending on location, market links, and other item-specific factors. The borrowing-financing operations of larger farmers and organized producers were also cut off or severely clipped. The impact was visible in different segments. Workers on plantations, such as rubber, tea, jute, and cardamom, were not paid wages. The small and medium tea growers had few buyers (a third of the tea was unsold in a recent auction in South India). Raw jute trade was halted as paucity of funds affects procurement delivery by traders. Projections of scarcity appeared with appeals for official procurement support. Cotton production and sale witnessed havoc: daily arrivals had plunged to 30,000 to 40,000 bales against the usual 1.5 to 2 lakh bales at the harvest time as per reports and prices had soared 9 percent in a week, pushing up global prices in turn. Vegetable and fruit sale that, along with crops, added 61 percent of agriculture's gross value-added in 2015 to 2016, depended critically on a cash-strapped transport sector for daily supply network. Sales have dropped sharply (25 to 50 percent) across markets with occurrences of dumping. Demand was found to be repressed for want of currency, so prices were subdued, but, eventually, supply shortages could cause prices to rise. Thus, price and output effects reflected all the factors. This means considerable fluctuations and increased uncertainty and risk (Kohli 2016). Farmers' unrest across states, including Madhya Pradesh, Rajasthan, and Maharashtra, turned into generalized agrarian distress over mounting debts, and the lines between what demonetization had done and what was due to long-running factors got blurred.

In sum, demonetization aggravated the existing stress points in the agriculture sector by creating new choke points within the supply chain. Cash is a critical input in the agricultural production process and its unexpected shortage had an impact at many levels, including a slowdown in the employment of labor and a dip in the overall farm incomes. The Economic Survey for 2016 to 2017 also echoed these concerns at that time (Singhal 2018). There are two types of impacts on agriculture: short term and long term. In the short term, as cash is the primary mode of transaction in the agriculture sector, demonetization is bound to cause temporary stress in the system. In the transitional phase, farm produces with limited shelf life, like fruits and vegetables, which significantly contribute to overall farm output, are hit due to the absence of cash. Similarly, the payment of wages to farm laborers and rentals for farm implements too become difficult considering the limited access of service providers to the banking system. So, basically, the Indian agriculture sector had to go through a rough time. As for the long-term impact, demonetization can affect agriculture directly in four ways. These include area sown, crop pattern, productivity, and market. This move has the potential of bringing about transformational changes in the sector like better access to credit for farmers; elimination of middlemen, which is one of the major causes of poor condition of Indian farmers as their profit is immensely reduced due to the commission of the middlemen; direct transfer of subsidies to farmers; and ultimately, linking the Indian farmer to the global agricultural market. If the Indian farmers are linked to the global market, it could generate a great amount of revenues for the country.

India's agricultural sector provides more jobs and sustainable incomes than all other sectors put together. Agriculture has shown strong resilience to the effect of demonetization. The sector has to brave several storms before it realizes the true fruits of demonetization. If demonetization engineers a transformation of the financial landscape in a way that farmers are integrated into the formal banking system, this could hold benefits in the long run in ways that may counterbalance short-term losses. Whether or how much farmer welfare is impacted remains to be seen. A market-driven, intense farming practice is a must for bringing about positive change on ground.

## Impact on Informal Sector and MSMEs

In an informal economy, an economic activity is neither taxed nor monitored by the government, in contrast to a formal economy. The informal sector is labor intensive, and thus not included in the government's gross national product (GNP). Informal economic activity is a dynamic process, which includes many aspects of economic and social theory, including exchange, regulation, and enforcement. The MSMEs sector is a big chunk of the economy, and its importance cannot be overstated. According to the estimates of the Ministry of MSMEs, the sector generates around 100 million jobs through over 46 million units. With 38 percent contribution to the nation's GDP, 40 percent to overall exports, and 45 percent of manufacturing output, they clearly form the backbone of the economy.

"This has resulted in varying degrees of disruption in the supply chain of business of all sizes" (Nanavati 2017). The MSMEs have been hugely impacted by demonetization as liquidity of currency has been severely affected. Many MSMEs found themselves without working capital. The sudden downturn in orders caused the more fragile enterprises to suspend operations or even to shut down. There is no clear indication as to the extent of this problem due to the difficulty of obtaining precise data about the functioning of India's informal sector or its smaller enterprises. But the numbers issued by industry associations or by bodies like the Centre for Monitoring the Indian Economy (CMIE) are far from encouraging. Demonetization has pulled down the growth of the MSME sector. The informal economy in India has varied reasons for being inaccessible to the government's net of regulation.

It can be presumed that the impact of demonetization on MSMEs will be higher than on the rest of the economy due to their greater dependence on hard cash. Their unvirtuous cash cycle begins from an expense base that is almost exclusively cash based. This then incentivizes the business to earn revenues in cash as well. The MSMEs are often managed by individual proprietors with small turnovers, limited reserves, and access to finance. In the short term, a significant reduction in job growth for non-skilled workers adds to the woes of labor-intensive industries and services, such as construction and retail trade. Sectors within the MSMEs space, like restaurants and transport operators, have also been negatively impacted since economic activity has declined and also due to the fact that there is a high tendency in this segment to accept payments through cash only.

However, demonetization has spurred a major change in the way MSMEs conduct business. Recognizing the need to relieve some of the pressure on MSMEs brought on by demonetization, the government appeared to make MSMEs a priority in the budgetary allocations for 2017 to 2018. These budgetary announcements were generally well received by MSMEs, reflecting hopes that they would lead to better infrastructure and a formalization of financial services. MSMEs are past masters and have always managed to find a way to beat taxes and licenses. The key methodology was to tempt officials with doles of various kinds (Beyes and Bhattacharya 2017). In a way, demonetization will help the organized MSMEs probably at the cost of the unorganized MSMEs. MSMEs and businesses now by design will have two options. Pay tax or spend on doing more for scaling up, and this will have a spiral effect on the overall improvement in the economy. Most bulk and regular purchases were anyway routed through the formal banking system. According to a Crisil's survey, nearly half of the MSMEs with annual turnover less than ₹ 2 crore reported a greater shift toward less cash, compared with a third of those with revenue over ₹ 25 crore (Mirchandani 2017). The substantial shift in traditional, cash-intensive sectors, such as textiles, electrical equipment, steel, and agricultural products, will "eventually transform business models in the MSME sector."

Despite the fact that 93 percent of labor force is in the informal sector, only 800,000 of the 59 million enterprises in India are registered as companies. These workers are overworked and underpaid, and the enterprises contribute nothing to the tax kitty. Moving the economic activity from informal to formal, despite the short-term pain of transition, is desired. "The government, instead of being defensive about demonetization, should stand up and say, yes, we meant well, but though the scheme didn't go as expected, it did have positive outcomes" (Ramesh 2018).

## Impact on Real Estate

As an asset class, real estate has been a big source of generating and consuming black money. The cash component in real estate has been there at various levels, beginning with land transactions, where it amounts to 30 to 50 percent. The cash payout is quite high in luxury housing too. The consumption of cash has been as high as 30 percent in secondary market transactions. The primary market transactions, however, are by far bereft of cash component as home purchases are financed through loans from banks and housing finance corporations. It is another matter that even in primary market deals, developers have been encouraging cash payouts by luring property buyers with good discounts on property price. The speculative buying by investors through offerings like underwriting and pre-launches has also been involving cash payout, leading to artificial price hike and, in turn, making homes out of the reach of masses.

Demonetization badly affected the liquidity in the capital-intensive real estate sector, deepening the problem of massive fund shortage/cash crunch faced by developers reeling under delayed deliveries, which deterred buyers from purchasing property. The impact was more evident in markets like the NCR and Mumbai, which were largely investor driven, compared to southern markets of Bengaluru and Chennai and even Pune in the west, which have been end-user driven. The premium/luxury residential segment, in which the cash component was more in transactions, got impacted by demonetization (Behl 2017).

The real estate and property prices are largely expected to fall, especially for sales of properties where the major part of the transaction is cash based, rather than based on bank transfer or check transactions. In the medium term, however, the prices in this sector could regain some levels as developers rebalance their prices (probably charging more on check payment).

Real estate experts' belief that the impact of demonetization is only short term and will not have the long-term impact stems from the fact that developers who have been following transparent and fair practices have not been affected by demonetization. One key positive impact of demonetization has been the enactment of the Real Estate Regulation Act (RERA), after which speculative investors deserted real estate, and end users/genuine buyers, who were all these years pushed to the sidelines, came out in large numbers. Now, it is the consumers who are driving the real estate market, especially residential market, aided by the government's pro-industry and pro-consumer initiatives. The step to promote affordable housing and according real estate industry status for the purpose of making easy and cheap funds available to the sector also helps.

Demonetization has particularly boosted foreign funding. The transparency brought in by demonetization, aided by RERA, GST reforms, and liberalization of FDI norms, has boosted the confidence of foreign investors. This will inject the much-needed liquidity into the sector starved of funds. Targeting consumers, the government under the Pradhan Mantri Awas Yojana (PMAY) is providing substantial interest subsidy to home buyers. The clampdown on floating cash in the system has contributed significantly to curbing inflation, which, in turn, helped RBI in cutting interest rates, thereby boosting home buying.

In short, it is expected that demonetization had a salutary impact on property prices by curbing cash transactions and checking speculative pricing, in turn increasing affordability, which is a key to achieve the government's flagship mission of "Housing for All." Demonetization, aided by other reforms like the *Benami* Property Act, RERA, and GST, will create institutional and regulatory framework for speedy and steady growth of the economy. These policy initiatives will help make real estate more organized, transparent, credible, and affordable, making the sector investor and consumer friendly. In the context of fungibility between cash and real estate, demonetization marked a material and discernible trend break.

As per the Colliers Research, the demonetization wave seems to have settled down and the prospect for the real estate sector looks promising in the long term.[1]

## Impact on Labor and Employment

Economic activity was disrupted due to demonetization and GST. According to CMIE, 1.538 million jobs were *lost* between September to December 2016 and January to April 2017 (Vyas 2017). Since consumer demand has slowed and consequently industrial production has declined, employment generation has been adversely impacted by the currency demonetization drive; not only fewer jobs are being created but layoffs also taking place. Was demonetization a demand-side shock to the system or a supply-side shock? Questions such as these continue to bother economist (Bakshi 2017). According to him, it was a demand-side shock to the economy and dealt a severe blow to hopes of a consumption-oriented recovery. But some experts contend otherwise. Pronab Sen (former chief statistician) was of the view that "by virtually killing of credit from informal sources of finance, demonetization was both a supply and demand side shock for the informal sector. For the corporate sector, though, it was a demand-side shock." Madan Sabnavis holds the same view and has observed that "while demonetization was a demand shock, it was a supply shock for the MSMEs." Some economists have argued the rise in imports during this period can be attributed to a fall in production due to the disruption caused by demonetization to domestic supply chains. But the demonetization-induced demand shock to the system should have dissipated as remonetization gathered steam. But during this period, the economy faced another disruption—the GST. GST is a supply-side shock for the corporate as well as the informal sector. It has also caused massive disruption in trade. This indicates demand is still a laggard in the system. The government's response should be to boost employment in the informal sector. The focus should be on programs such as rural roads, housing, and minor irrigation projects that encourage labor-intensive work. Gradually, with supportive policies, the gains will overtake the pain (Bakshi 2017).

Demonetization had a major impact on the labor market and has resulted in increased uncertainty and a fall in employment elasticity. Demonetization was instituted in a context in which a majority of workers are paid in cash and have no written contracts or benefits. The effects have been felt in both the formal and informal economies. This base-of-the-pyramid workforce was the sector most impacted by demonetization. On the labor front there may be some longer term pain. Smaller businesses are dependent on migrant labor, which is frequently moving across India. Many of these workers either do not have proper IDs or have IDs that are not valid in the state in which they work. The lack of income in the immediate aftermath of demonetization forced them out, thus hurting the business continuity. Further, as revenue transactions come into the white sphere, businesses will be forced to change the mindset of labor and help ease their financial inclusion, which will not be easy (Nanavati 2017). After demonetization, the female labor participation rate fell by 4.93 percentage points in just 1 year. It fell from 16.37 to 11.44 percent in May to August 2017. Male labor force participation rate fell by a lower 2.5 percentage points, from 74.76 to 72.33 percent during the same period. Many leave the labor markets when they lose hope (Vyas 2018).

## Impact on Digital Transaction Systems

This section attempts to understand whether demonetization has pushed India toward a more formal and digital economy. On the positive side, there is likely to be a reset of spending patterns as this move represents indirectly a significant push toward a cashless economy. Businesses in the fintech sector, including payment banks, mobile wallets, electronic transfer providers, etc., are expected to see gains. With cash transactions facing a reduction, alternative forms of payment have seen a surge in the demand. Digital transaction systems, e-wallets and apps, online transactions using e-banking, usage of plastic money (debit and credit cards), etc. will definitely see substantial increase in demand. This should eventually lead to strengthening of such systems. This has been seen as one of the driving factors to propose this change. The demonetization drive could be seen as a blessing for India's move toward a cashless economy and for encouraging consumers to use digital payment platforms. It also supports the government's Digital India initiative, which aims to encourage cashless payment solutions across the country by putting the technological infrastructure in place.

As per the RBI report, at the end of March 2017, the cash-to-GDP ratio was 8.8 percent, down from 12.2 percent in 2016. At this level, India's currency-to-GDP ratio compares well with a host of advanced and emerging market economies (such as Germany, France, Italy, Thailand, and Malaysia).[2] The cash culture in India is dominant and people prefer to use cash wherever possible. Currently, businesses from street-side stalls to wholesalers rekindle their love for cash. Now traders say they are operating much as they did before the ban, with cash once again the king. This is how business is done in India. It depends how closely the government monitors this (also see Chapter 12).

## Impact on the Financial Sector

Demonetization had a positive impact on financialization of household savings in India. It led to several changes for the financial sector, which are as follows (Singh et al. 2017):

    I.  Shift in currency demand;
   II.  Significant growth in bank deposits;
  III.  Greater financial inclusion;
  IV.  Detection of suspicious transactions;
   V.  Improved monetary transmission;
  VI.  Increase in mutual fund investments by households;
 VII.  Higher collections under life insurance schemes;
VIII.  Accelerated digitization of retail payments; and
  IX.  Higher rate of detection of fake Indian currency notes (FICNs).

If there is one sector that has done particularly well as a result of demonetization, it is the banking sector. It has led to more amounts being deposited in savings and current account of commercial banks. Excess deposit growth in the banking system during the period of demonetization up to the end of March 2017 would be in the range of 3.0 to 3.8 percentage points. In nominal terms, excess deposits accrued to the banking system due to demonetization are estimated in the range of ₹ 2.8 to ₹ 4.3 trillion. The unusual cash deposit in specific accounts, which are usually less active, is estimated to be in the range of ₹ 1.6 to ₹ 1.7 trillion. Overall, there appears to have been a significant increase in bank deposits due to demonetization, which if sustained, could have a favorable impact on financial savings and their channelization to capital markets. The financial markets have not shown the drastic volatile behavior. The demonetization drive has been successful in making the banking sector healthier. The shift in savings behavior is starkest when evaluated in terms of the savings mix—physical versus financial savings. Households save in both financial products (bank deposits, insurance, mutual funds, equities, etc.) and physical products (primarily real estate). For only the second time in nearly two decades, the share of financial savings outstripped physical savings in the financial year 2017. This, of course, can be attributed to multiple reasons—the slowdown in real estate being a crucial one—but the trend break on account of demonetization has been rather stark to be merely a coincidence (Mukherjee 2018). Former RBI deputy governor S. S. Mundra was of the view that people could have factored in a rise in interest rates and, therefore, did not want to lock in their savings for longer durations. Such instances also happen when people plan to move to other asset classes and not depend on bank fixed deposits. Since demonetization was not a usual phenomenon, the behavior of depositors cannot be compared to the previous years (Ghosh 2018).

Household financial savings that had been stuck at 10 percent range of gross national disposable income (GNDI) for a long time had perked up by a full 1 to 11.8 percent for the financial year ending March 2017. The big shift has been in deposits, as can be expected post-demonetization. But there has also been a massive shift in the "shares, debenture and mutual funds" category, from 0.3 to 1.2 percent. Micro-level data on mutual funds, alternative investment funds (AIF), and portfolio management services (PMS) flow suggest that there has been an even greater pickup in flows in the financial year 2018. Total assets under management (AUM) of mutual funds grew from ₹ 16 lakh crore in October 2016 (before demonetization) to ₹ 23 lakh crore, a growth of nearly 50 percent. A very large number of new investors in mutual fund have come from what are described as Class B and C cities/towns in the country, reflecting the emergence of a new generation and class of financial market participants.

It is important to note what the financial sector saw post demonetization wasn't a one-time event, but a structural breakout that has deepened and widened the financial market in India. Both the key outcomes—greater financialization of savings and the shift within financial savings to capital market instruments (equities, bonds, mutual funds)—have a far-reaching impact in the manner in which India funds its growth. For example, systematic investment plans (SIPs) in mutual funds, whose numbers and value went up dramatically after demonetization, generate domestic equity flows of ₹ 5,000 to ₹ 6,000 crore every month, or ₹ 75,000 crore every year. That is greater than the quantum of foreign institutional investors (FIIs) flows typically in a normal good year. By itself, such a large captive source of risk capital throws up interesting opportunities for businesses looking to fund their investment plans (Mukherjee 2018).

## Impact on Government Revenues

The demonetization drive has the potential to raise government revenue. It is expected to boost government revenue to the extent that helps to move economic activity from the informal to the formal sector. The impact of demonetization on union government accounts was mainly on the tax revenue collection. In addition, the Income Tax Department also dovetailed its Operation Clean Money in February 2017. By August 2017, data analytics by the Income Tax department resulted in ₹ 15,496 crore being surrendered as undisclosed income and another ₹ 13,920 crore coming in by way of seizures. Further, 14,000 properties, each valued more than ₹ 1 crore, are currently under scrutiny as owners have not filed income tax returns. Furthermore, there has been an increase of about 25 percent in income tax returns filed during the fiscal year 2016 to 2017, and an estimated 2.1 lakh shell firms have already been deregistered. However, it is important to note that the average income level of the new taxpayers was ₹ 2.7 lakh, slightly above the tax threshold. So, the new people brought under the tax net are not the superrich who have been evading tax all these years. They are more likely to be relatively small people who have come under the tax net because of pressure from the banks to link accounts with the *Aadhaar card* and the PAN card and the GST bringing some people in. So, it is not that fat cats were disgorging their illicit hoards due to demonetization.[3]

The high growth in income tax returns and the GST inflows indicated that more and more people now preferred to undertake "white money" transactions. On property taxes, some local bodies have given people a window of opportunity to pay old as well as current taxes in the scrapped notes. This has resulted in an increase in revenue collections in property tax. The government cannot expect to get major collections in terms of the tax and penalty on unaccounted incomes revealed. The digital push of the government will also result in higher indirect tax revenue in the form of service tax. Moreover, businesses that underreported their revenue earlier will have to make proper disclosure, especially of revenue received through digital or cashless means.

The priority is to ensure compliance by those who pose a large risk of revenue leakage to the exchequer. Tax compliance is definitely improving as the data collected by the government after demonetization acts as a deterrent. The safeguard needed here is to ensure that to the extent possible this vast data is used carefully and does not result in inquiries that are avoidable. The impact of demonetization can be seen in the surge in PAN registrations. From around 2.7 million registrations in November 2016, the number went up to 9.6 million in April 2017.[4]

One of the promises of demonetization was a rapid expansion in the tax base, but the actual results have been quite modest. The tax base expansion attributable to demonetization was ₹ 10,600 crore, equivalent to only 0.1 percent of India's GDP. The full effect on tax collections will materialize gradually as reported income of new taxpayers will grow. *In sum*, the tax revenue has improved, which favors the positive impact of demonetization. But based on ratio terms, the tax revenue receipts have not increased considerably, and hence, demonetization has not had much impact (Nataraj 2017). Some believe that the increase in compliance, which would rake in higher revenues year after year, is even better than the onetime bumper harvest the scheme aimed for (Ramesh 2018).

## Impact on Political Parties

The pernicious practice of political parties *buying votes* with cash hand-outs during elections is probably the area where demonetization might have its largest effect in the short term since this requires hoarding of cash. While every country has its share of corrupt politicians, it is this corruption that is endemic in Indian society. This group of individuals might have a harder time laundering their cash holdings. Demonetization has stunned political parties. Cash donations are a huge part of "election management." In one stroke, big parties will find themselves hamstrung as cash hoards are often undeclared money. Parties will have to completely rejig their strategies in light of cash crunch. Donations to political parties have also been brought within the ambit of formal banking.

## Impact on Other Economic Entities

Like any other sector, the industrial, logistics, and warehousing sectors went through a slump over an initial couple of months owing to the cash crunch brought along with demonetization. However, of late, the growth of the sectors has been accelerated with the rollout of the GST. There will be welfare loss for the currency-using population. Most active segments of the population who constitute the "base of the pyramid" use currency to meet their transactions. Those in the unorganized sectors, like carpenters, utility service providers, etc., faced short-term disruptions in facilitation of their transactions. Similarly, roadside vendors, cab drivers, grocery stores, etc. felt the pinch in the beginning. Some of the most common areas in the services sector where undisclosed income is utilized are the entertainment, hotels and restaurants, tourism, etc. These segments had to face the most significant impact because the nature, frequency, and amounts of the commercial transactions involved with these sections of the economy necessitate cash transactions on a more frequent basis. Sometimes, a deflationary situation cannot also be neglected, which will hamper the economy.

The aftereffects have also taken some time to feed through the system. In its latest Article IV Consultation report on India, released in

August 2018, the International Monetary Fund (IMF) has observed: "The impact on growth appears to have been more severe and longer-lasting than anticipated at the time of the 2017 Article IV *Consultation* with a disproportionate impact on the informal sector." The impact was felt both at the firm level as well as at the consumer level. The disruption caused by cash shortages dampened consumer and business sentiments, leading to a decline in high-frequency consumption and production indicators, such as sales of two-wheelers and cement output, respectively (Singhal 2018).

There has been disproportionate impact of this policy on the middle- and lower-wage classes, and it is the derailment of the latter's lives that has caused many to write that the policy is a failure and others to go so far as to call it a criminal injustice. It is the vast majority of India, which the government wants to help with the recovered black money that is actually paying the heaviest price for this policy. Demonetization did more harm to the economy and certainly did not make a big dent on corruption or black money. There are loads of positive and negative impacts of demonetization. As it is a move that is unprecedented in terms of scale, it is extremely difficult even for experts to make a quick judgment on its possible outcome.[5]

Demonetization has changed consumer behavior in both good and bad ways. The flows into the equity markets should help drive savings growth for Indians over the long term. It has also helped in understanding the weaknesses of the currency circulation systems and steps are being taken to fix these. Importantly, however, there are many long-term benefits, which cannot be evaluated in rupee terms. For example, there is immense value attached to the intangibles, such as credible threat to forgery rackets and enhancing the national security milieu, a shift in the people's mindset in favor of digital payments, a shift in the propensity of the informal sector to get into formal one, and the potential increase in tax base to finance public goods. Such long-term benefits are impossible to be captured in the current estimates of the GDP growth rates (Deodhar 2017). Demonetization was a gamble fraught with unknowns, and it should be seen as part of several reforms. It is not enough to judge the efficacy and impact of such a measure on the economy and on the behavioral dynamics of people at least in the short run.

## Endnotes

1. https://housing.com/news/one-year-since-demonetzation-real-estate-outlook-positive-colliers-international/, (accessed September 28, 2018).
2. *Financial Express*, Online, August 31, 2017.
3. In an Interview with Pranab Bardhan by Devadeep Purohit, *The Telegraph*, January 22, 2018.
4. Tighter Scrutiny after Demonetization Led to Rise in PAN Registrations, ITR Filings, *MINT*, November 6, 2017.
5. https://www.go4hosting.in/blog/sme/how-has-demonetization-impacted-small-medium-businesses-in-india, (accessed January 16, 2019).

# CHAPTER 11

# Demonetization and Black Economy

There is a widespread misconception that the phenomenon of black economy is unique to the Indian setting and that the rest of the world, particularly the advanced capitalist countries of Europe and North America, are free from it. A large body of work of scholars like *Friedrich Schneider*, who noted with the help of global data that the phenomenon is by no means absent in those regions, may provide some comfort to Indian readers (Nayak 2017a). Parallel economy or black economy exists in both developed and developing countries. The term *black economy* is variously referred to as hidden economy, illegal economy, phantom trades, shadow economy, subterranean economy, unaccounted economy, unregulated economy, unreported economy, and unsanctioned economy.

The problem of the black economy in India is old and deep rooted. The black money has been troubling India, particularly since before Independence. The fungibility of the black money reveals that over seven decades, the parallel economy has so spectacularly permeated life that it has got completely intertwined with the formal economy. At one stroke, demonetization has choked the supply of black money stacked inside the country. It is true that those who had bought land and housing property, gold and jewelry, art treasures, etc. using black money could not be penalized by the demonetization process. Demonetization is a deep psychological strike on black money. It was a very good signaling device that the government was very serious about cracking down on corruption and black money.

## Concept of Black Money

To begin with, let us see the nature of black money, the sources of its generation, the forms in which it is held, and the means of mitigating it. Black money refers to assets or resources that have been neither reported to the public authorities at the time of their generation nor disclosed at any point of time during their possession (GoI 2012). According to Deodhar (2017), black money is a catchall phrase that represents the value of four kinds of transactions:

I. Transactions that are either unreported or underreported to evade taxes—leading to lower government revenues, higher fiscal deficit, and/or inadequate delivery of public infrastructure.

II. Corruption, that is, money that changes hand to curry favors in business deals and skirt administrative rules, resulting in allocation of contracts to inefficient firms, violation of safety and sustainability rules, and distribution of income in favor of certain personnel.

III. Transactions carried out in illegal goods, such as narcotics, liquor, weapons, and human trafficking, which are welfare reducing and remain unreported.

IV. Payments for financing terror attacks and "stone pelting" to destabilize country using counterfeit currency.

According to J. C. Sandesara, "in popular parlance, the unofficial economy goes by the name of black money and the official of white money. Black and white is also variously substituted by number two and number one, unaccounted and accounted, unreported and reported, unrecorded and recorded and so on."[1] An equally important fact is that black money is a flow, not a stock, meaning that it cannot be captured, accounted for, and eliminated in one stroke. It is crucial to make a clear distinction between black income, a flow concept, and black wealth, which may be held in the form of currency, a stock concept. The term "black money," or *kala dhan*, is often confusingly used to refer to both black income and black wealth. One may define black income as that income.

I. Which is illegal,

II. Which evades tax, or

III. Which escapes inclusion in national income estimates (Nayak 2017a).

Thus, according to Lahiri (2016), the term "black money," in popular parlance, is used to refer to three distinct categories—black wealth, black income, and black currency, the term "black" connoting its "illegal" or unaccounted nature. "Black wealth" is several times more than black income—it is what has been accumulated from black income over several years. And black income is several times more than black currency. Black income can be earned even without the use of currency, for example, with gold or diamonds.

It is a fact that much of the underground economy is cash based. Illegal activities, in particular, such as accepting bribes, including those given to political parties as "donations"; drug trafficking; prostitution; bootlegging; and gambling, involve transactions in cash. Unreported income from lawful activities, such as legal and medical counseling; from tips; from work by household and farm help; and from independent contracting, also tend to be in cash. The black component of currency is that part of currency that has just mediated a black transaction and is still with the perpetrator. The universal acceptability of cash; the convenience in storing, moving, and hiding it; and the associated anonymity are the factors that lead one to use it for such purposes. Even within currency notes, high-denomination notes are the preferred medium of transaction.

## Estimates of Black Economy

An abundance of literature is available on measurement techniques and estimates of parallel economy. A variety of methods have been used, which appear to generate widely divergent estimates. There is no clear data on the quantum of black money in the Indian economy. Black incomes largely come from factor incomes and property incomes that are not reported to the direct tax authorities. Depending on the definition used, one would obtain alternative estimates of the extent of the black economy. There are four major ways of computing black income:

   I. The survey method
  II. The input–output method
 III. The monetarist approach
 IV. The fiscal approach

Various authors, committees, and institutions have used the monetary approach, the currency demand approach, and the fiscal approach. While the method most widely used globally is the monetarist approach, the one most commonly used in India is the fiscal approach, which was propounded in the 1950s by the Cambridge economist Nicholas Kaldor (Nayak 2017a).

For understanding how large the black money market in India is, one has to make the distinction between black currency, black economy (GDP), and black wealth. In one of its pioneering studies, the National Institute of Public Finance and Policy (NIPFP) put the extent of the black economy in India at 18 to 21 percent of the GDP, computed with 1983 to 1984 data. It is entirely possible that the extent of the black economy may well have increased significantly over the past three decades, largely owing to the growth of the services sector and the phenomenon of over- and under-invoicing in foreign trade. Kumar (2016) has asserted that at present, the black economy is estimated to be 62 percent of the GDP. Currency is more important in the black economy than in the overall economy. Black wealth would be higher since it is accumulated over time. Given that black wealth includes both cash holdings and gold and real estate, it is likely to be higher since the latter two have much lower rates of depreciation. In other words, black wealth compared to the economy's measured GDP might be very high.

Estimates of black money in India fluctuate wildly. A World Bank report puts India's shadow economy at close to one-fifth of economic output. Another study on illicit financial flows by Global Financial Integrity (GFI) puts these at 3 percent of economic output for India between 2002 and 2011. This difficulty in measurement is because black money is generated through a raft of complex, sophisticated activities for the purposes of tax evasion, crime, and corruption. A part of the generation of black money is on the part of professionals, for example, accountants, doctors, and lawyers. Some studies exclude certain sources of black money. The GFI excludes criminal activities and a part of corporate tax evasion, both massive sources of black money. Hence, its estimates are naturally more conservative (Singh 2014). Thus, reliable estimates are hard to come by and also depend on whether one is talking about the shadow economy. In India, black money refers not only to this but also to bribes used to receive government services as well as the cash that is used to purchase votes during elections.

The previous UPA government commissioned three institutes to estimate the quantum of black money. The studies were conducted by the Delhi-based National Institute of Public Finance and Policy (NIPFP) and the National Council of Applied Economic Research (NCAER), and the Faridabad-based National Institute of Financial Management (NIFM). The NIPFP, NCAER, and NIFM reports were received by the government on December 30, 2013; July 18, 2014; and August 21, 2014, respectively. The government is still examining these three reports and that information on the findings of the reports was "exempt from disclosure" under the RTI Act as they were under examination and were yet to be taken to the Parliament.[2] More than 4 years have elapsed and the government has not yet decided to place it before the Parliament. But unofficial sources reveal that the NIPFP-estimated "black money" in 2012 was of the magnitude of 75 percent of the GDP. And much of it is held in the form of gold, real estate, land, shares, and stocks, while some of it is kept in tax havens through shell companies that make its detection difficult. Thus, there is a feeling among scholars that most of the black money generated in India is no more in Swiss banks. Black money or unaccounted money is the result of deficiencies in the tax administration of the government. The typical black marketer is very much part of the banking system. The huge size of the Indian underground economy is difficult to fathom. A fair amount of India's black money is stashed outside the country as well.

The Union Finance Ministry's White Paper on Black Money (2012) spells out in detail the manner in which the black economy is generated in India. However, this detailed document does not point to the cash

economy as the cause for the black economy, though it does make the
point that it is "related." The paper also makes it evident that black money
is the *effect* of other causes, which need to be addressed. Black income
is kept in the form of physical assets like gold, land, buildings, etc. This
makes it inherently difficult to measure black money accurately. Table 11.1
summarizes the estimates made by scholars at different points of time.

*Table 11.1  Estimates of black economy in India (using fiscal
approach)*

| Year | Black Economy/GDP | Estimated By |
|------|-------------------|--------------|
| (1) | (2) | (3) |
| 1956 | 4.5 | Kaldor (1956) |
| 1970 | 7 | Wanchoo Committee (1970) |
| 1976–77 | 10.2 | Chopra (1982) |
| 1980–81 to 1983 | 18 to 21 | NIPFP (1985) |
| 1980–81 | 15 | Basu (1995) |
| 1990–91 | 35 | Kumar (1999) |
| 1995–96 | 40 | Kumar (1999) |
| 2013 | 75 | NIPFP (2013) |

*Sources:* Kumar (2016b) and Ghandy (2016).

It is clear from the above that there have been estimates of the black
economy and the "black money" generated in the country from time to
time. Like the national income, the estimates of "black money" refer to the
sum generated in an accounting year. Since it is not a stock, black money
generated in 1 year may find ways of investment or use as white money in
the successive transactions. Since accounting of all the shadow activities is
by certain attributed values, the estimates could vary widely.[3] According
to some estimates, only about 6 to 10 percent of the "black money" is held
in the form of cash.[4] "Black money" is a continuous flow in the illegal and
legal activities that are part of the socioeconomic system. Illegal sources of
black money that escape the tax network include smuggling, bootlegging,
trafficking in drugs, and sex- and crime-related extortions. Estimates suggest that criminal and illegal sources account for only a fraction of the total
black money flow in the economy, while almost three-fourths are generated from the legal production, services, financial, and trade activities.

## Causes of Generation of Black Money in India

Black money is accumulated through different sources. The three main sources of black money are corruption, *hawala,* and crime. Among these, corruption is the chief villain. Hoarding cash at home is common in most Indian households. But the roots of the generation of black money in India are different. *In general,* monumental amassing of ill-gotten wealth through corruption was invested in shell companies, mines, an island off-shore of India, real estate, sponge iron plants, private colleges, transport and trucking, hotels, theme park, distilleries, print media, and TV channels. Much of the corrupt black money amassed thus flows out as white. And this raises the question whether the Prime Minister was setting an agenda to unearth black money and check corruption through demon-etization (Reddy 2017b). In sum, the main sources of black money are:

    I. Higher tax rates, large-scale tax evasion, and ineffective enforce-ment of tax laws;
    II. Controls and licensing system, widespread corruption, and graft of various kinds to secure political or administrative goodwill;
    III. Commodities, stocks, and *benami* transactions;
    IV. Foreign trade transactions: deliberate "mispricing" or "misinvoic-ing," cost manipulation, and manipulation of wage data;
    V. Investment in real estates;
    VI. Private educational societies;
    VII. Nongovernmental organizations (NGO);
    VIII. Cooperative banks, which do not fall under the purview of the RBI;
    IX. Underreporting of production;
    X. Agricultural income;
    XI. Funding of political parties; and
    XII. Other factors:activities like smuggling; concealment of income by professionals, artists, etc.; and privatization.

## Foreign Trade Transactions

One of the important factors generating "black money" is mispricing (over-invoicing of imports and under-invoicing of exports), which is difficult to estimate. "Trade misinvoicing" or over-invoicing of imports and under-invoicing of exports involve falsifying the values listed on commercial invoices. This is an extraordinarily common tool by which corporations and individuals in developing countries avoid import or export tariffs, alter their income tax positions, evade foreign exchange controls, or simply move their wealth to developed countries or tax havens. "Trade misinvoicing" is also a common method of shifting the proceeds of crime or corruption and is typically referred to in these cases as trade-based money laundering. Deliberate "mispricing" or "misinvoicing" takes two forms, namely, "under-invoicing of exports," which hides part of the export earnings retained in undisclosed foreign accounts, and underreporting of export earnings that shows lower profits, resulting in tax avoidance in the domestic country. Similarly, "over-invoicing of imports" would show an inflated domestic cost of production and reduced profits in the balance sheet, evading domestic taxes to that extent. In addition, inflated payments shown for imports are retained in undisclosed foreign accounts.[5]

According to one report, in 2014, India accounted for half of global "mispricing" disputes. The available estimates by GFI show that between 2003 and 2012, India accounted for a cumulative illicit outflow of about $440 billion, or about ₹ 30 lakh crores, which works out to an average annual outflow of about $44 billion, or ₹ 3 lakh crores. All this is described as "black money," and none of it is in Indian currency or in Indian accounts. What is important to note is that those involved in illicit financial outflows that get parked abroad are not content with the "black money" that hardly earns any returns in the tax havens. They would like to "round route" it as white money for making profits in the domestic financial markets or stock exchanges. Round routing of the spoils of illicit financial earnings made by "misinvoicing," *hawala*, or other routes of money laundering came back as white money in the Indian financial markets through shell companies in several tax havens, including Mauritius, Singapore, and Cyprus (Reddy 2017b).

## Hawala and Crime

*Hawala* works by transferring money without actually moving it. "*White hawala*" is used to refer to legitimate transactions. "*Black hawala*" refers to illegitimate transactions, specifically hawala money laundering (associated with some serious offense such as narcotics trafficking and fraud). In the case of India, Interpol estimates the size of hawala at possibly 40 percent of the country's GDP. Criminal offense includes drug trafficking, gunrunning, money laundering and extortion, murder for hire, fraud, human trafficking, poaching, and prostitution. Many criminal operations engage in black markets, political violence, religiously motivated violence, terrorism, and abduction. Other crimes are homicide, robbery, assault, etc. Property crimes include burglary, theft, motor vehicle theft, and arson. Demonetization will be effective to the extent that these activities are carried out with Indian high-denominated currencies. A sizeable volume of business is done by way of high-denominated currencies, though no scientific data is available in this respect.[6]

## Black Money kept Abroad

Much of the black money held abroad was round routed into the Indian stock exchanges through *promissory notes* (PNs) bought in Mauritius through front shell companies. A substantial proportion of FII investments were made through the PN route. It was well known that almost all FIIs were running subaccounts for dubious clients, but repeated RBI warnings against it were ignored. In all this, there is hardly any hard cash involved, nor is there any accumulation in the Indian banks, but in offshore banks. In this context, the important point to note is that the process is such that demonetization will not be able to curb this.

The data leak that reveals the global trail of many Indian corporates in tax havens is a great victory for transparency. The *Paradise Paper* reported 714 Indian names, including that of a top doctor who got shares from the very firms whose stents he was using. This is the largest ever leak of financial data featuring 19 global tax havens, which help the global rich and powerful to come up with complex offshore structures to dodge tax—underlines yet again the severe challenges in combating tax evasion. Setting up offshore entities is not always illegal, but as the *Paradise Papers* show, very often the motives were shadowy. Illegal or not, the likes of *Paradise Papers* expose various deals/connections that the layperson wouldn't normally even imagine. As for governments with such information public, even if they want to help cover up, they would be hard pressed to explain why they took no action (Sarin et al. 2017).

Government had initiated a multi-agency probe to investigate the list of Indians named. However, tax avoidance in deals is often seen by tax authorities as strictly legal in form, but perhaps not in substance. The Shome Committee considered tax avoidance as a "gray area." Policies fail both at the macro-level and at the micro-level. Targets for education, health, drinking water, etc. are not achieved because "expenditures do not mean outcomes." Much investment goes into wasteful and unproductive channels (Kumar 2011).

## Impulsive Behavior and Rise of Crony Capitalism

The magnitude of black money has increased during economic reforms of 1990s. In the name of competition, efficiency, liberalization, and privatization, it is ironical that what emerged was neither competition nor efficiency, but "crony capitalism," which could acquire hugely valuable natural resources dirt cheap in the name of priority allotments and access to contracts for infrastructure projects and telecommunications. Socially critical public goods like education and health became the most sought-after avenues for private profit. The clamor was that state should withdraw from direct economic activities and create a regulatory system that would govern the private sector. This reform approach gave birth to extensive "crony capitalism" with powerful self-interested actors gaining control over the state to their advantage, a process that has come to be known as "state capture" or "regulatory capture." Crony capitalism gains the ability to get the laws consciously "adjusted" to its advantage and to the detriment of the public good. "When business interests succeed in shaping the legal, political or regulatory environment to suit their own interests and distort public policies, it would provide unlimited opportunities for corruption. Thus, economic reforms and the resulting "crony capitalism" are at the root of the eruption of corruption as "grand scams" that has come to occupy the public notion of corruption and revulsion to those associated with it" (Reddy 2017b).

## Corruption

The nature of some businesses is such that they need to do transaction in cash. Take an example of a business that does transactions entirely in white despite the large cash outgoes on expenses. When a rent seeker like a factory/ labor inspector, excise official, or policeman comes by and demands a payout, the business is forced to set aside some cash to service these payments. The most convenient way is not to account for some revenue, which also saves tax and provides the needed hard cash. The expenditure of such nature is regarded more as a cost of convenience and is one of the main roots of the black economy. Also, many businesses depend on customers who preferred to pay in cash. This was a key demand driver for many small manufacturing and trading businesses. In general, MSME entrepreneurs are a master at this art. They were quick to spot ways to get through with the compliances and taxes, and the officials were happy to receive the unaccounted benefits. Soon, it was also noted that the return on investment on taxes paid was meager, and there always were alternatives available to a frugal mindset. This gave rise to the parallel economy of black money. It's a classic case of poor processes at the government level. Processes are always interlinked, and therefore, while constructing them, one has to look at all the sub-processes they will impact.[7]

The ranking of countries in terms of their cash-to-GDP ratios (as on June 29, 2017, in Rogoff's The Curse of Cash) provides important information. It is not correct to say that countries with a lower cash-to-GDP ratio are less corrupt while those with a higher ratio have a greater the potential for corruption. The country with the highest cash-to-GDP ratio is Japan with a figure of 19.40 percent. It also happens to be one of the least corrupt. Whereas in Nigeria, the cash-to-GDP ratio is very low, at 1.55 percent, but it is one of the world's most corrupt countries. According to the same ranking, Singapore, Switzerland, Hong Kong, and the whole of the Eurozone have cash-to-GDP ratios significantly above India's, also significantly less corrupt. On the other hand, Argentina, Colombia, South Africa, and Brazil have cash-to-GDP ratios that are around half of or even lesser than India's, but they are perceived to be as corrupt as India. Thus, the truth is the cash-to-GDP ratio is not a test of corruption or corruptibility because how much cash one holds doesn't make or tempt one to be corrupt. What matters is the character of the people handling cash and what they do with it. That, in turn, is determined by the incentives or disincentives to encourage or deter corruption. Regardless of what cash-to-GDP ratio is or might become, the system encourages corruption. This is the core problem that has still to be tackled (Thapar 2017).

Prior to 1991, there was widespread corruption at the top, middle, and bottom levels of governance in India. Economic reforms could be a source of huge one-time rents to politicians in power, for example, privatization of public monopolies. This reduces their ability to use the public sector for political patronage in the future. The sources of corruption can be traced to scarcity, property rights and their enforcement, transaction costs and information asymmetries, and political position (Patibandla and Sanyal 2009). Corruption through scarcity is generally seen in terms of a mismatch between demand and supply. In the case of goods, the market structure of an industry (monopoly versus competition), price regulation, quantity limits, zoning, and differential tax treatment in different states results in scarcity, which creates opportunities for rent (corruption). In the case of service sector, a supplier or a government body may refuse to provide a service, unless a bribe is paid. In the post-reform era, some sources of scarcity-related corruption have been magnified, owing to weak property rights and high transaction costs of enforcement. As a result, corruption has been part of the society, including the pre-reform period. There are sectors that lead to unreported income or profits from privatized public goods like education and health services, which have emerged as a large source of "black money" flow through unreported capitation and other charges (Reddy 2017b).

*In sum*, hoards of cash, particularly high-value notes, are acquired in a variety of businesses that go into financing the informal sector. There are a number of intermediaries in the fishing, agricultural, and service sectors with unaccounted money in currency form. Arresting this phenomenon will be beneficial to the society. There are black money and black income, and there are corruption and bribery. These go hand in hand most of the times, but not always. Black income is surprisingly not very high in India since a large part of the Indian economy is not taxed. This sort of black cash has become not just a part of the economy, but a dynamic part at that.

## Demonetization Does Little to Curb Black Money

A fraction of the high-value notes are not being used for transactions but rather for storing black money. There has been skepticism over the ability of demonetization to make a dent on the black economy because currency is a poor store of value. As there are other options to hold black money, it is not surprising that less than 10 percent of India's black economy is held in the form of cash. The black money holder is a prudent manager of wealth and would not choose to park it as cash. This is not merely out of the fear of getting caught, but for more economic and practical reasons, such as the debilitating inflation and the existence of alternative asset classes, for instance, real estate, jewelry, and bullion that offer safer store of value. Shourie[8] is of the view that this policy is not poking on black money because the owner of black money converted their money into tangible and intangible assets. Improved information about the cash economy requires information on wealth of the richest, which is sparse. In India, very little is known about hidden wealth. The pattern of deposits should provide the government information about those who might have potentially laundered their black money and information on the various channels and modes through which black money operates. This assumes that the government has the expertise, human resources, and conviction to follow up. Further, if corruption itself cannot be addressed, then one may very well end up with a scenario where new black money will drive out old black money from the system. Despite voicing noble intentions and the expectations raised, there is little that has been delivered in terms of ridding the economy of black money through demonetization.[9]

The government move is against illegal wealth rather than illegal income—the stock rather than the flow. The problem lies in the overuse of cash in economic transactions. Higher cash usage in India is because of a combination of factors—the parallel economy, a large informal sector, high inflation, and rising rural wages. The government perceives corruption primarily as a cash-based issue. However, cash is only a small part of the Indian shadow economy, which includes, but is not limited, to income from corrupt practices.

The people who are best equipped to avoid the intended trap of demonetization are precisely the ones who are seasoned dealers in black money.[10] Indians are experts at circumventing laws and regulation. There is a term for it—*jugaad*.[11] The measure by itself will not have any impact on the incentives to generate black money, and it does not deter earning illegal incomes and evade taxes. This being the reason, economists are divided especially on the question of whether a one-time penalty on un-declared cash hoardings is likely to curb the future flow and accumulation of black money. However, the big painful jolt of demonetization creates the right psychological milieu for the war against black money (Lahiri 2016). How the government balances the twin objectives of unearthing black money and safeguarding innocents from mistreatment is something to watch out for. The problem is that many people look at demonetiza-tion in isolation. In reality, for the government, it was only one in a series of steps meant to reduce black money and corruption that have moved wheels in India for too long.

Long-term benefits of demonetization will depend on "the implemen-tation of other government policies to fight black money and corrup-tion and how well it succeeds in accelerating progress towards financial inclusion. For example, India's new Goods and Services Tax may make tax enforcement somewhat easier, and the government has been engaging in financial information treaties with other countries to make offshore laundering more difficult" (Rogoff 2016). Rogoff's perceptive analysis is very instructive when he opined that "perhaps surprisingly, India's de-monetization, no matter how much criticized by economists, has been broadly popular in a country where people are deeply frustrated by en-demic corruption, and appreciate the government's broad efforts to fight it. Certainly demonetization has greatly accelerated financial inclusion, with hundreds of millions of Indians now taking advantage of heavily subsidized basic debit accounts, a program that until now, had been de-veloping relatively slowly. There is little doubt that multitudes of papers will be written on India's demonetization, but it could take years to un-tangle its full effects, which have as much to do with psychology as eco-nomics".[12] What happens in the future cannot be known, of course, but an attempt has been made.

## Post-demonetization: The Steps Taken by the Government

Despite the concern of the union government about the prevalence of the black money and setting up of various commissions for controlling it, results are not so impressive. The government has decided to address the bigger issue of corruption and black money in a comprehensive way, covering both short- and long-term measures. Demonetization was a corrective step, and irresponsible monetary management is being stopped. It follows a number of other steps that were aimed at cornering and identifying those who deal in black money. The authorities claim that demonetization succeeded in unearthing black money and preventing corruption. The Parliament was informed that data analytics was being used to match information in IT returns with cash deposit data and identify high-risk cases/groups for necessary verification/investigation.[13] The paybacks of enhanced transparency were visible when on the basis of data mined after demonetization, the Ministry of Corporate Affairs (MCA) struck off around 2.24 lakh companies for remaining inactive for a period of 2 years or more. Several of these companies are suspected to be shell companies, and restrictions have been imposed on the operation of their bank accounts and sale of movable and immovable properties until they are restored. Shell companies are also used for fictitious transactions aimed at inflating expenses by larger companies as well as by promoters of companies with large public interest to divert funds to privately held entities.

The government is trying to identify instances of money laundering by shell companies and is seeking help from state authorities to prevent transfer of properties belonging to these companies, some of which have been deregistered for failing to comply with regulatory requirements. State governments have been advised to disallow registration of properties of such entities. Although the shell companies are struck off from the registry, liability for any offense committed will still rest with the officers responsible for statutory compliance, and with promoters. In similar but separate action, around 3.09 lakh board of directors were disqualified for their companies failing to file financial statements and/or annual reports for a continuous period of three financial years, necessary under the Companies Act 2013. The MCA claimed that it has taken several steps to end the practice of dummy directors, including seeding Director Identification Number (DIN) with Permanent Account Number (PAN) and *Aadhaar* at the time of DIN application through biometric matching for new applications.[14]

Demonetization has strengthened tax administrative measures against black money. It has fortified the tax administrators' tools, interventions, and interactions with the taxpayers by producing greater compliance. Continued stress on digital payment, deregistering of shell companies, and a sharp focus on *benami* properties point to such an approach. The indirect working of the demonetization has been much stronger as it has strengthened the enforcement mechanism. Demonetization has propelled accessory program to fight black money. Alone, demonetization is weak, but together with these newly launched initiatives, it can create a compliant society. Other measures are more crucial, like bringing the offshore tax evaders to book those whose names figure in the Panama papers, conducting raid on *benami* properties, making donations to political parties open to public scrutiny, and making it mandatory for all donations above ₹ 2000 to political parties and religious places to be through digital means only. These measures have reduced the circumference of the parallel economy.

Demonetization has made a social shake-up of Indian society for detaching practices related to black money. The biggest contribution of demonetization is its campaign value as a nationwide awareness program against black money. This will help India to create a compliant and transparent society. Further, in the light of the evidence with respect to the abuse of the corporate structure through multi-layering, not more than two layers are now permitted beyond the wholly owned subsidiary.[15] Demonetization cannot and will not prevent future generation of black money since the black money problem is more of a cultural mindset in India than a legal problem. Black money can be eliminated only if there is a change in the mentality of the public. The attitude of people should change against black money. The awareness of the drawback of black money can eliminate it. Demonetization will require a wholesale rethink by participants in the parallel economy. Businesses need to think about *first* entering the banking system, *second* digitizing, and *third* full declaration. Big resets to practices and mindsets will need to happen (Nanavati 2017). Ending black money calls for a larger change in governance practices, attitudes, and habits. This means root-and-branch overhaul in the society to defeat black money. Electoral, political, judicial, and administrative reforms besides systemic reforms need to take place. The government needs to remain focused on ensuring that the desired outcomes are delivered. Only then one can hope for truly transformational days to come. Whether demonetization turns out to be a transformative measure that delivered substantial long-term benefits and whether those benefits were worth the short-term pain is too early to judge. A more balanced evaluation is called for. But on the whole, the demonetization exercise as it stands today appears to have been a bold experiment, which went through peacefully, though the results are still unclear.

## Endnotes

1. https://www.ijasrd.org/wp-content/uploads/2017/05/A-Study-on-Demonetization-and-Its-Impact-on-Cashless-Transactions.pdf (accessed October 10, 2018).
2. Examining reports on black money commissioned by UPA: Arun Jaitely, The Indian Express, September 20, 2017.
3. Hiding in the Shadows https://www.imf.org/external/pubs/ft/issues/issues30/ (accessed October 10, 2018).
4. Only 6–10 percent of the black money is kept in cash, News headline, The Times of India , November 12, 2016.
5. What is trade misinvoicing? https://www.indianeconomy.net/splclassroom/what-is-trade-misinvoicing/ (accessed October 12, 2018).
6. Black money, corruption, and demonetization by Dr. Martin Patrick, November 10, 2016. https://www.cppr.in/article/black-money-corruption-and-demonetization/ (accessed October 14, 2018).
7. How demonetization has impacted the Indian SME https://yourstory.com/2016/11/demonetization-impact-indian-sme/ (accessed October 10, 2018).
8. In an interview with NDTV, October 3, 2017.
9. https://www.thehinducentre.com/multimedia/archive/03153/Background_Note_No_3153982a.pdf (accessed October 18, 2018).
10. Interview: Demonetization move declares all Indians as possible crooks, unless they can establish otherwise, say Amartya Sen https://www.reddit.com/r/india/comments/5exo31/interview_demonetization_move_declares_all/ (accessed October 14, 2018).

11. Jugaad has many meanings—finding a makeshift, low-cost, or creative solution to a problem; being entrepreneurial and innovative; removing obstacles; or troubleshooting. This may also be construed as innovation. Jugaadu is used to describe someone adept at jugaad, and is almost always treated as a compliment.

12. What on earth was India thinking when it banned the $7.50 bill? https://www.pbs.org/newshour/economy/hell-india-thinking-banned-7-50-bill (accessed October 16, 2018).

13. DeMo succeeded in unearthing black money, preventing corruption: FM http://news.rediff.com/commentary/2018/mar/22/liveupdates .htm (accessed October 16, 2018).

14. Govt cancelled 2.24 lakh suspected shell companies post demonetization disqualified 3.09 lakh directors https://www.firstpost.com/ business/govt-cancelled-2-24-lakh-suspected-shell-companies-post-demonetization-disqualified-3-09-lakh-directors-4194085.html (accessed October 16, 2018).

15. Deregistered firms deposited Rs 17,000 crore post note ban, The Indian Express, November 6, 2017.

# CHAPTER 12

# Demonetization as a Move to a Less-Cash Economy

In a country whose economy was dominated by cash transactions, demonetization was a drastic attempt to change the behavior of Indians, moving them away from the use of currency notes toward electronic modes of transferring money. However, cash still remains the oxygen of the Indian economy. Given the magnitude of informal sectors in Indian economy, unreported tax-liable income earned in cash even in the pursuit of legitimate activity is likely substantial. Taking into account the economy's move toward less-cash economy, this chapter seeks to deal with the following issues:

   I. Concept of cashless transaction
   II. Rationale behind a less-cash economy
  III. Use of cash in the United States and the United Kingdom
  IV. Policy measures taken for a less-cash economy
   V. Challenges in moving toward a less-cash economy
  VI. Conditions needed for the success of less-cash transactions
 VII. Ensuring behavioral change

## The Concept of Cashless Transaction

A cashless transaction connotes an economic state whereby financial transactions are not conducted with money in the form of physical banknotes or coins, but rather through the transfer of digital information (usually an electronic representation of money) between the transacting parties. However, the focus is on an economy where cash is replaced by its digital equivalent—in other words, legal tender (money), is recorded and is exchanged only in an electronic digital form. The point to be noted is that "a cashless economy is a system where flow of cash or physical currency is non-existent and all monetary transactions are done electronically via internet enabled banking or wallets and debit or credit cards, at most abolishing or at times reducing physical presence between two transacting parties. Such transactions can be purchases, bill and utility payments and clearances or transfers."[1] The aim is to minimize the circulation of physical currency as India uses too much cash for transactions.

## Rationale behind Less-cash Transaction

There are several reasons why the government and the RBI bring up measures to promote cashless transaction in the economy. It is a universally accepted fact that a cashless economy is good for growth. Several studies have indicated that the alternative methods for money transfer and payments benefit all players in the ecosystem—the government, central bank, commercial banks, the industry, and the consumers (Kinger 2016). In India, such a move was considered to help the government and the RBI reduce operational costs resulting from managing cash and preventing counterfeit currency use. It can also help enhance financial inclusion, check tax evasion, and improve collections. Here, the terms *less cash society* and *cashless-transaction economy* indicate one and the same thing—reducing cash transactions and settlement rather than doing transactions digitally. Cashless transaction economy doesn't mean shortage of cash; rather, it indicates a culture of people settling transactions digitally. In a modern economy, money moves electronically. Hence, the spread of digital payment culture, along with the expansion of infrastructure facilities, is needed to achieve the goal. The main merits of cashless transactions are as follows:

I. Reduced instances of tax avoidance and money laundering because transaction trails are left in financial institutions-based economy, thanks to the higher traceability of all the transactions in the economy, allowing more transparency in business operations and money transfers. The resulting transparency will change the way of thinking about regulation and compliance.

II. Cash transactions were tools for unscrupulous parties to refrain from paying the necessary taxes and duties. This will bring more transactions in the market under the supervision of the government. It will curb the generation of black money.

III. A cashless society relying on digital payments could, over time, enhance the usage of financial services by those parts of the population that have no formal access to banks; at the same time, going cashless could address the economic and security problems usually associated with cash.

IV. It will reduce real estate prices because of curbs on black money as most of the black money is invested in real estate, which inflates the prices of real estate markets.

V. It will pave way for the universal availability of banking services to all as no physical infrastructure is needed other than digital.

VI. There will be greater efficiency in welfare programs as money is wired directly into the accounts of recipients. Thus, once money is transferred directly into a beneficiary's bank account, the entire process becomes transparent. Payments can be easily traced and collected, and corruption will automatically drop, so people will no longer have to pay to collect what is rightfully theirs.

VII. There will be improvement in credit access and financial inclusion, which will benefit the growth of MSMEs in the medium/long run.

VIII. No scope for fake currency will remain. In India, 1 in 7 notes is supposed to be fake, which has a huge negative impact on the economy; by going cashless, that can be avoided. In a cashless economy, there will be no problem of soiled notes or counterfeit currency.

IX. There will be efficiency gains as transaction costs across the economy would also come down. The increased use of credit/debit cards will definitely lessen the need for carrying cash resulting in curtailing the risk and the cost associated with that. In addition, it also reduces cost of printing currency.

X. Data procurement and use for policy making are important because more accurate data shall improve GDP calculation. Better policy and planning by monitoring consumption and expenditure patterns would be possible.

Rogoff offers the rationale for the merits of a "less-cash" economy. But small-denomination notes have to be available indefinitely. Despite its usefulness, using this system and eliminating the cash system require a number of policy changes. The eventual achievement of a cashless state is a very complex task and seems to be a distant dream. There are merits and demerits for both cash and digital transactions. The most common risk in cash transactions is that of counterfeiting of currency. However, the cost of a cash transaction is the lowest.

## Use of Cash in the United Kingdom and the United States[2]

The world as a whole will go cashless, but predicting the same for any country is very difficult because cash is fighting back. People are paying more and more by card and phone, but the amount of cash in circulation continues to climb in just about every country, except Sweden. In 2017, the UK had more than £73 billion (about ₹ 67,000 crore) worth of notes in circulation—up from £67,819 million in 2016. That is much faster than inflation and growth combined and works out to be more than £1,100 per person. The number for the U.S. dollars was even more stunning. There are some $1.6 trillion notes in circulation, which on a quick tally is $5,000 per person in America. The U.S. dollar continues to be the preferred medium of exchange for the global drug-dealing community, but it is used around the world for quite legitimate transactions as well. The U.S. dollar has become virtually the international currency. The Euro, too, has a growing international presence, which explains why there is the equivalent of €3,300 (about ₹ 2.6 lakh) in circulation for every person living in the Eurozone. In Germany, cards are nudging out cash. According to the Bundes bank, in 2017, for the first time, cash accounted for less than half of all transactions by volume. On the one hand, there is a steady shift away from using cash across the developed world. On the other, there is an apparently insatiable demand for more banknotes to be printed.

There is probably some reaction too against the tracked economy. Some people, particularly those who have money, prefer not to have every payment they receive or make recorded on a bank or social network computer. But the number of those who are against tracking would have to be huge to account for the increase in the use of banknotes.

## The Policy Measures taken for Less-cash Economy

In India, the RBI and the government are making several efforts to reduce the use of cash in the economy by promoting the digital/payment devices, including prepaid instruments and cards. RBI's effort to encourage these new varieties of payment and settlement facilities aims to achieve the goal of a "less cash" society. In October 2012, the RBI had used the phrase "less cash"—and set it as its goal—for the first time in its 2012 to 2015 vision document for payment systems in the country. The RBI unveiled a document in June 2016—"Payments and Settlement Systems in India: Vision 2018"—setting out a plan to encourage electronic payments and to enable India to move toward a cashless economy in the medium and long term. The broad contours of Vision 2018 revolve around *five* Cs— coverage, convenience, confidence, convergence, and cost. To achieve these, Vision 2018 focuses on four strategic initiatives: responsive regulation, robust infrastructure, effective supervision, and customer centricity.[3] The vision statement highlights the following plans:

A)  To reduce the share of paper-based clearing instruments
B)  To raise the growth of the digital payments space
C)  To ensure the accelerated use of *Aadhaar* in payment systems

The Telecom Regulatory Authority of India (TRAI) is helping a drive toward the adoption of mobile payments. It has recently published a consulting paper on the review of the regulatory framework for the use of the Unstructured Supplementary Service Data (USSD) technology for mobile financial services.[4] This model for financial inclusion has been extremely successful in countries like Kenya, where the m-Pesa mobile money transfer has become the de facto standard for e-payments. After the growth of Internet banking and payments through NEFT, RTGS, and immediate payment service (IMPS), some recent policy decisions and program rolled out to help facilitate increase of noncash transactions. The government made fiscal measures for the encouragement of card culture in the 2016 budget. Exempting service charge on card-based and other digital payments was one such step. *Aadhaar*-based payment system will be a big boost for promoting the cashless transaction culture.

Soon after demonetization, the Ratan Watal committee on digital payments submitted its report.[5]Another committee of chief ministers was set up by the Niti Aayog under Andhra Pradesh chief minister N. Chandrababu Naidu, which has come up with an action plan to rapidly expand the use of digital payment platforms across the country. This committee spawned another committee for digital payments security under IT secretary Aruna Sundararajan. Niti Aayog has set up another committee helmed by chief executive officer Amitabh Kant to "enable 100 percent conversion of government-citizen transactions to the digital platform." Meanwhile, the Ministry of Electronics and Information Technology (MEITY) has issued its own guidelines to facilitate the adoption of electronic payments and receipts for various government services. Demonetization also occasioned a host of other private reports. Such a surfeit of committees and reports has led to overlaps and repetitions (Singhal 2017).

India joined "Better than Cash Alliance (BTCA)" on September 1, 2015. In BTCA's own words, its new partnership with India is an extension of the Indian government's commitment to reduce cash in its economy. A less-cash economy means that money can finally flow into bank accounts, heralding a new era where subsidies can directly be deposited into the bank accounts of the poor as the aim is to protect the common man.

Post demonetization, the government has developed secure platforms for money transfer and encouraged private players in the financial space, including banks, to roll out e-payment services with adequate security features. The state-promoted unified payments interface (UPI) has seen rapid adoption over the past 2 years. Other payment modes, such as credit and debit cards, unstructured supplementary service data, prepaid payment instruments, and Internet banking, have also witnessed a surge in the number of users. To push digital payments further, the government has also decided to waive off the merchant discount rates applicable on debit cards, BHIM, UPI, and *Aadhaar*-enabled payments system of up to

₹ 2,000 for 2 years with effect from January 1, 2018. The center aims to grow India's digital economy to $1 trillion by 2022 (Gupta 2018).

## Challenges in Moving toward a Less-cash Economy

The inhibitions against adopting cashless transactions in India are mirrored in multiple issues. For digital payments, key issues are a higher risk of frauds, higher transaction cost (each transaction), and lack of privacy. In view of this, some major challenges in promoting a digital economy in the country relate to:

  I.  Attitudinal factors,
 II.  Infrastructure,
III.  Data connectivity,
 IV.  Cyber-security,
  V.  A higher cost of digital transactions as compared to cash transactions, etc.
 VI.  Micro-aspects, which create a number of challenges as follows:
      A.  Availability of Internet connection and financial literacy.
      B.  Most of the *Jan Dhan Yojana*, which is lying nonoperational; unless people start operating bank accounts, cashless economy is not possible.
      C.  Some vested interest in not moving toward a cashless economy.
      D.  Small retailers who dominate India; they don't have enough resources and will to invest in electronic payment infrastructure.
      E.  The perception of consumers, which also sometimes acts as a barrier; the benefit of cashless transactions is not evident to even those who have credit/debit cards, and it is generally accepted that having cash helps to negotiate better.[6]
      F.  The cost of providing equipment in remote parts of the country and ensuring seamless connectivity at an affordable cost.

While reducing cash transactions in the economy, it is equally important to protect consumers and businesses from frauds that can happen on electronic and digital platforms. The major factor is trust.

The increasing number of reports of online fraud and data breaches has heightened consumer worries. The trust factor extends beyond digital payments as well. India has experienced a number of prominent e-commerce frauds where customers have received something other than what they ordered. A poor telecom network only aggravates these issues. Cyber-security is a major concern, and there are many legal and practical problems and regulatory issues connected to it. All these problems will be magnified many times in small towns and villages. Cashless transactions are still rarely used in rural areas and in the informal sector, like roadside vendors; small shops; seeds, fruits, and vegetables sellers; wage payments in the informal sector; etc.[7] *In short*, there are a number of transition challenges that need to be managed (Mishra 2016):

I. **Infrastructure issues:** There is a need for a significant upgrade of the banking system as well in the telecom infrastructure to provide the backbone for digital transactions. It is important that not only the banking system is upgraded to ensure that transactions can be completed without a hitch but that the supporting infrastructure is also up to the mark.

II. **Consumer behavior issues:** A behavioral change is being expected in people from using cash as a medium of exchange to using other cash substitutes both for making and for receiving payments. This transition requires individuals to make two changes in their behavior: one, agents need to move from tangible means, which can be seen and felt, to forms, which are less tangible or not tangible; and second, they have to learn to rely on technologically advanced tools to undertake regular day-to-day operations. The latter requires agents to be educated to the extent of comprehending the content of transactions. If this transition is not suitably managed, agents might be tempted to move to nonofficial cash substitutes.

III. **Accessibility in language:** Most of the banks and the mobile instruments for transaction are currently adapted to a single to two languages. If the bulk of the population of this country needs to come on board, it might be important to make these facilities available in different Indian languages to ensure that the user can comprehend the transaction that they are entering into.

## Prerequisites of the Success of Less-cash Transactions

Transition to a cashless economy depends on a number of factors:

I.  There has to be the availability of a quality telecom network.

II.  Banks and related service providers will have to constantly invest in technology in order to improve security and ease of transaction. People will only shift when it's easier, certain, and safe to make cashless transactions.

III.  The government will have to find ways to incentivize cashless trans-actions and discourage cash payments. The government will have to create conditions.

IV.  Companies, customers, and the government should collectively participate to mitigate cyber-attacks and minimize its damages. The push for digitization cannot be at the cost of the digital security of its citizens. The government must work on putting fire walls in place.

V.  The *Watal* committee has suggested strengthening of existing laws to protect consumers and their privacy. It has also recommended an independent payments regulator within the framework of the RBI and similar treatment for banks and nonbanking entities in the payments space.

VI.  There is a need to develop connectivity infrastructure parallel to the cashless push. More open platforms like UPI that have an interop-erable framework are also important.

VII.  Electronic payments have to be easy to adopt. There are plenty of models around the world to learn from. In some countries today, person-to-person payments are generally made digitally. If the gov-ernment wishes to push faster for a cashless economy, policy and regulation need to focus on competition and innovation.

VIII.  There is a need to leverage a low-cost transaction enabler with a ubiquitous payment–network–operator business model. Mass adoption of such a model can definitely solve some of the major issues associated with going cashless. Only when a laborer is able to digitize his or her transactions, be it daily wages or in payment for even a small purchase, one will realize the cashless vision.

IX. The RBI will have to come to terms with a few issues, from figuring out what digital payments across borders mean for its capital controls to how the new modes of payment affect key monetary variables, such as the velocity of money.[8]

The demonetization drive is not only about curbing black money but also about combating cash. Along with political pressure, outreach and initiatives at the grassroots level are the need of the hour. A pragmatic approach has to be swiftly put in place to educate and empower people to fend from being cheated. Right now, there is a need for financial and digital literacy. RBI should ensure the printing and supply of currency to every nook and corner of the country, in the denomination desired. The consequences of going in for a cashless dispensation by fiat/coercion will not be good for the economy. Further, incentives for moving to electronic transactions and lucky draws alone won't suffice.

A majority of people do not use a bank for financial transactions not because of the physical distance from a bank branch but because of a psychological distance. The drive toward cashless India could further increase the "class divide" among the banked and unbanked in India. There is a risk of creating islands, where the unbanked transact with each other. This divide could seriously affect the government's financial inclusion initiatives (Dominic 2017). The Jan Dhan scheme promotes financial inclusion, but it is not actively being used. Barriers to behavior change were lowered immediately after demonetization. The human brain loves the *status quo*. The common man experiences no problems while transacting in cash. Systems and infrastructure should be in place before a behavior-change initiative can begin. Even if the infrastructure is in place, there is no guarantee that the right behavior will take root. Getting people to use the infrastructure on a sustained basis is a different issue.

Making India cashless is not a single-event change project. Shifting to a digital format requires a sustained behavior change. There is a lesson to learn from the cash crunch of March to April 2018. Given the continuing nature of overwhelming cash transactions, the economy needs more cash, and it is for the RBI to balance the requirements, which admirably serves the purpose. There is a fear among people over the availability of cash, and there could be a tendency of small businesses withdrawing money and hoarding cash given that bank credit is not easily available to them.

The pace of growth in digital transactions was higher as long as the effects of demonetization affected currency circulation. However, the demonetization move paved the way for digital payments and transactions in a big way. More Indians from smaller towns and cities are paying digitally for goods and services, raising expectations of sustained growth for noncash payments. There is a general increase in the usage of cards for smaller-value transactions, which is a clear indication of the fact that it is eating into cash payments. Industry experts said that while debit card transactions may be slowing, more people are using newer modes of digital payments for daily purchases. As merchants started accepting wallets like *Paytm* or *PhonePe* for digital transactions, the trend has shifted and a lot of small-value retail payments could have moved away from cards. Visa and Mastercard are losing market share in India to indigenously developed payment systems of UPI and RuPay Card.

The shift to digital payments has also been boosted by the rapid expansion of the UPI. National Payments Corporation of India (NPCI), which manages the platform, recorded 482 million UPI transactions in October 2018 as against 0.2 million in November 2016. What demonetization has done for digital payments is more than what any other initiative could achieve before.[9]

Therefore, different trajectories need to be planned for migration to cashless for those having a bank account and for those not having one. In this context, socioeconomic factors would need to be considered. It may be helpful if a long-term plan with cost implications and with a stipulated timeline is prepared to decide on various aspects of building a cashless economy. Given India's poor financial infrastructure, this could not be achieved in haste. Instead, it is prudent to follow an incremental approach toward creating a digital transformation in the economy.

## Endnotes

1. "Unified Payment Interface—A Step towards a Cashless Economy." https://abhimanuias.com/blogs/Important-Issues-DetailedArticle /7645 (accessed October 8, 2018).

2. The Tribune. 2018. "Online Payments Rise, but Cash Stays On," Homson Reuters Foundation, The Independent, London. https://www.tribuneindia.com/news/sunday-special/perspective/online-payments-rise-but-cash-stays-on/570293.html (accessed October 8, 2018).

3. Payment and Settlement Systems in India: Vision-2018, RBI, June 23, 2016.

4. Trai Seeks Ways to Boost Telcos' USSD Channel for Financial Inclusion, *The Economic Times*, August 3, 2016.

5. Repot of the Committee on Digital Payments, Ministry of Finance, GoI, December 2016.

6. Insights. 2015. "Insights into Editorial: Making the Transition to a Cashless Economy + Mindmaps on Issues." http://www.insightsonindia.com/2015/11/17/insights-into-editorial-making-the-transition-to-a-cashless-economy-mindmaps-on-issues (accessed October 10, 2018).

7. IAS Cracker. 2018. "Impact of Currency Demonetization on the Indian Economy." https://iaskracker.com/currency-demonetisation-impact/ (accessed October 8, 2018).

8. Insights. 2015. "Insights into Editorial: Making the Transition to a Cashless Economy + Mindmaps on Issues." http://www.insightsonindia.com/2015/11/17/insights-into-editorial-making-the-transition-to-a-cashless-economy-mindmaps-on-issues (accessed October 10, 2018).

9. Demonetization Impact: Bharat Going Digital for Payments, Newspaper Headline, *The Economic Times*, November 9, 2018.

# CHAPTER 13

# Relation between Union Government and the Reserve Bank of India

In every country, there is one organization that works as the central bank. The function of the central bank of a country is to control and monitor the banking and financial system of the country. The Reserve Bank of India (RBI) is the central bank of the Indian financial system. The enactment of the Reserve Bank of India Act, 1934 paved the way for setting up the system. The RBI was established on April 1, 1935. In the earlier years, it did not have adequate powers of control or regulation. This Act gave the RBI powers to regulate issue of banknotes, the custody of the commercial banks' cash reserves, and the discretion of granting them accommodation. Some promotional role was envisaged for the RBI from the very beginning as agricultural credit was its special responsibility in terms of the RBI Act. RBI was nationalized in the year 1949 and became a government-owned institution under the Reserve Bank Act, of 1948, which empowered the central government to issue directions to the bank, after consultation with the governor of the bank. The general superintendence and direction of the bank are entrusted to the 21-member Central Board of Directors.

## Functions of the RBI

There are two broad categories of functions of the RBI:

  I.  Conventional or monetary functions and
  II. Promotional or nonmonetary functions.

Monetary functions are also known as the central banking functions of the RBI; they are related to control and regulation of money and credit, that is, issue of currency, control of bank credit, control of foreign exchange operations, and banker to the government and to the money market. Monetary functions of the RBI are significant as they control and regulate the volume of money and credit in the country.

Equally important, however, are the nonmonetary functions of the RBI in the context of India's economic development. The supervisory function of the RBI may be regarded as a nonmonetary function (though many consider this a monetary function). The promotion of a sound banking system in India is an important goal of the RBI. The RBI has been given wide and drastic powers, under the Banking Regulation Act of 1949—these powers relate to licensing of banks, branch expansion, liquidity of their assets, management and methods of working, inspection, amalgamation, reconstruction, and liquidation.

With economic growth, assuming a new urgency since Independence, the range of the RBI's functions has steadily widened. The bank now performs a variety of developmental and promotional functions, which, at one time, were regarded as outside the normal scope of central banking. Consequent upon the establishment of the National Bank for Agriculture and Rural Development (NABARD), the obligation cast on the RBI under Section 54 of the Reserve Bank of India Act in the sphere of agricultural credit has been considerably modified. The amended section envisages that the bank may maintain expert staff to study various aspects of rural credit and development, and, in particular, it may tender expert guidance and assistance to the NABARD and conduct special studies in such areas as it may consider necessary for promoting integrated rural development.

## Importance of RBI

It is almost 84 years since the RBI was established. During this period, the range of functions of the bank has steadily expanded from discharging the traditional central banking and regulatory functions for securing monetary stability to taking on an active developmental and promotional role to meet the demands and needs of a developing economy. The bank was instrumental in establishing several specialized financial institutions, which has gone a long way in the mobilization of savings of the community and capital formation. Concurrently with the promotional stance, the bank was engaged in the task of maintaining stability in an era of rapid economic development ushered in with the launching of the 5 Year Plans; additional powers of credit control were acquired and control techniques were adapted to suit the complex and changing economic situation.

The nationalization of the 14 major scheduled commercial banks in the private sector in July 1969 marked a watershed not only in the annals of Indian banking but also in the growth of the Bank's responsibilities, especially in the matter of extension of banking facilities in terms of their geographical coverage and directing the flow of credit to the neglected sectors of the economy. RBI undertakes several special functions aimed at developing the financial system such as: integrating the informal credit market into the organized financial sectors, encouraging innovation in cooperative banks and extension of the commercial banking system in the rural areas, and influencing the allocation of long-term investment credit. It also has a creative role in developing the system.

A notable legislative measure in the recent past (The Reserve Bank of India Amendment Act 2006) relates to greater flexibility to RBI in regard to cash reserve requirements, deployment of forex reserves and clarity in regulation over money, forex, and government securities markets. In the overall context of its policy and operations, the RBI, in practice, is subject to the current legal framework and operates as a monetary authority with multiple objectives and multiple functions assigned to it. In short, the role of RBI has been redefined through gradual evolution and adoptions along with some statutory changes, and not through any radical restructuring. Further, one should recognize that RBI is not a pure monetary authority, but is responsible for several other functions also, as a central bank. There are some constraints in the conduct of monetary policy, in particular, the fiscal impact, predominant public ownership, etc. While these challenges and dilemmas persist in the Indian context, every effort is made by RBI to meet the broader objectives set forth, from time to time.[1]

# Working of RBI (1950 to 2019)

In the first decade after independence, the edifice of central banking in India rested on four pillars:

I. Monetary policy,
II. Developing an orderly and well-regulated banking system,
III. Establishing and financing the infrastructure for agricultural credit, and
IV. Institutionalizing long-term lending to industry.

Not surprisingly, against the background of a rapidly liberalizing economy, *relations between the RBI and the government have also been changing.* A major development was a 1996 agreement limiting the monetization of government debt, which has helped increase elbow room for monetary policy. A central bank's independence is usually defined in relation to the government. However, in recent years, pressure has grown from other quarters to weaken or disperse the regulatory powers of the RBI, notably in the area of bank regulation.

The financial system in India is regulated by independent regulators in the field of banking, insurance, capital market, commodities market, and pension funds. However, the Government of India (GoI) plays a significant role in controlling the financial system in India and influences the roles of such regulators at least to some extent. At present, financial regulation in India is oriented toward *product regulation*; that is, each product is separately regulated. For example, fixed deposits and other banking products are regulated by the RBI, small savings products by the GoI, mutual funds and equity markets by the Securities and Exchange Board of India (SEBI), insurance by the Insurance Regulatory Development Authority of India (IRDA), and the New Pension Scheme (NPS) by the Pension Fund Regulatory and Development Authority (PFRDA). Each regulator has its own rules on registration, code of conduct, commissions, and fees to monitor the product providers and distributors.[2] The RBI has consumer price index (CPI)-based inflation growth targets to adhere to while deciding its monetary policy stance.

# RBI and the Demonetization

The governor told the parliamentary panel that the RBI accepted the government's proposal to recall ₹ 500 and ₹ 1,000 banknotes. The decision to demonetize was announced by Prime Minister Narendra Modi on November 8, 2016. Less than 4 hours before he announced demonetization, the RBI Central Board gave its approval to the scheme but also rejected, in writing, two of the key justifications—black money and counterfeit notes. The minutes of the 561st meeting of the RBI's Central Board, which was convened hurriedly in New Delhi at 5.30 p.m. that day, reveal that the central bank's directors described the move as "commendable" but also warned that demonetization "will have a short-term negative effect on the GDP for the current year." In its counter-argument, the RBI Central Board noted that "while any incidence of counterfeiting is a concern, ₹ 400 crore as a percentage of the total quantum of currency in circulation in the country is not very significant." The minutes include an "assurance" that the issue of demonetization was under discussion between the central government and the RBI for 6 months during which "most of the issues had been discussed." The RBI governor also recorded that apart from the stated objectives, the proposed step also presents a big opportunity to take the process of financial inclusion and incentivizing the use of electronic modes of payment forward as people can see the benefits of bank accounts and electronic means of payment overuse of cash.[3]

Demonetization is a part of monetary policy as it has directly affected the liquidity in the system. Also, the push for a cashless society, even as it has deep fiscal benefits, would help in improving the transmission mechanism and give the RBI better control over the supply of money and its movement thereof.

Government has the powers to declare legal tender illegal: Section 26 (2) of RBI Act gives this power on recommendation of the Central Board, the central government may, by notification in the Gazette of India, declare that, with effect from such date as may be specified in the notification, any series of bank notes of any denomination shall cease to be legal tender. So before any decision is taken, the Ministry of Finance had an important role to play in case of the recent demonetization. Overall one can say, the step to a certain extent was a well calculated one but the execution didn't go smooth. The work between November 8, 2016 (the date on which the currency ban was announced), and December 31, 2016, and even beyond, was being carried out by RBI. With tight deadlines, the RBI worked under enormous pressure to take back the banned notes after screening them and then quickly re-filed the system with new notes to ensure minimum hardship to people.

R. Gandhi (former Deputy Governor, RBI) has asserted that "the demonetization program had a detailed plan of action; large scale preparations preceded the commencement date; execution was to the script; and unanticipated mid-course corrections were minimal." Former RBI governor Raghuram Rajan was of the view that demonetization was "not a good idea" and that its implementation was "not well-planned" and "well thought-out" useful exercise. The current RBI governor Urjit Patel said that "the decision has not been taken in haste but after detailed deliberations. There had to be a high level of secrecy surrounding this decision and the fact is that such a large country was indeed taken by surprise when the decision was announced." In the foreword to the 14th Financial Stability Report (June 2017), Patel stated that "demonetization is expected to significantly transform the domestic economy in due course in terms of greater intermediation, efficiency gains, accountability and transparency through increasing adoption of digital modes of payments, notwithstanding the short-term disruptions in certain segments of the economy and public hardship." Thus, one can safely say that Patel has been largely a supporter of move unlike Rajan (Unnikrishnan 2018).

The extent of the RBI's role in shaping demonetization, in fact, caused significant discussion, including allegations that the policy had originated with the Prime Minister's office rather than the RBI, reducing the central bank's role to "rubber stamping." Some commentators have argued this damaged the long-term credibility of the RBI as an independent body and may further have violated Indian law (Kapadia 2016; Kumar 2016a). Y.V. Reddy talks about the thankless task the RBI was entrusted with in remonetizing the economy. He says "the task assigned to the RBI was such that great pain was, perhaps, inevitable." The way the whole exercise was designed and implemented put the RBI's reputation at great risk—"RBI's image has been dented, but not beyond repair."[4]

The RBI has transferred ₹ 306 billion of its surplus to the government for the financial year 2016 to 2017, less than half of the ₹ 6,508 billion it transferred a year earlier. However, it went up to ₹ 500 billion for the year ended June 30, 2018. Demonetization appears to be the spoiler-in-chief for the RBIs profit. The RBI did not provide any reason for the decline in dividend but this may be because of the cost incurred by the central bank in printing new notes as well as in sterilizing liquidity after old ₹ 500 and ₹ 1,000 currency notes were scrapped in November and subsequently returned to the banking system. RBI incurred a total expenditure of about ₹ 80 billion on printing currency notes in 2016 to 2017, which is more than double the ₹ 34 billion spent year before that. The rise in cost of printing could be attributed to printing of new currency notes during re-monetization. The upsurge in expenditure during the year was on account of change in the production plan of printing presses due to the introduction of new design notes in higher denominations as well as the requirement of larger volume of notes for replacement of the demonetized currency. The RBI, banks and the cash management companies learnt a lot from the demonetization exercise in 2016. RBI has constituted high-level committees and is aggressively implementing the recommendations to ensure the currency cycle in India is smooth and consumers can depend on access to their cash.

## The Question of RBI's Autonomy

Globally, the relationship between the central bank and the elected government has often been fraught. Friction between elected governments and central banks is not uncommon—be it on interest rate revisions or exchange rate management. India is no exception. Making an oft-argued case for central bank autonomy should surprise no one. Syncretic criticism is a part of the relationship. Currently, multiple flashpoints between the RBI and the government have led to grumbling between the two. RBI's key grievance appears to be on the government's frequent attempts to encroach on its turf. Tensions between the two have spilled over into areas such as regulation of banks and handling of bad loans, oversight of the payments system, transfer of surplus from the central bank to the government, and so on. While recognizing these inherent tensions, it is important that both sides tread carefully in their public exchanges. There are bigger battles to be fought, with external sector threats, such as multiple interest rate hikes in the United States and the fall-out of the trade war between the United States and China looming ahead. Macroeconomic stability is paramount given the threat of foreign portfolio outflows due to higher interest rates in the United States and geopolitical uncertainties, not to mention that worries overshadow banks creating ripples in the financial system. It may well be worth remembering that the India story is predicated not just on the country's economic prospects but also on having strong institutions. On this count, the government may keep in mind the RBI's impressive track record in steering monetary policy and India's financial sector over the past several years.[5]

RBI was set up 12 years before India's independence. In its more than eight decades of existence, it has distinguished itself with conduct of the highest standards. It is among a handful of national institutions known for exemplary integrity and incorruptibility. Of course, it may have had its share of bad apples and it may have committed policy mistakes (known only in hindsight). The main reason for central banks' independence is that governments are much more myopic, as political considerations are often short term (Ranade 2018). It is necessary for the government to respect the operational autonomy of the central bank. Undermining the ability of RBI to take decisions will affect market confidence and end up complicating the policy environment.

The government and the RBI should always get to the negotiating table. Dialogue is the best way to diffuse a "dispute," instead of using a brahmastra (Section 7 of the RBI Act) that is more effective as an unused deterrence. A central bank, in ensuring financial stability, has to perform adequately on multiple dimensions, and has to be flexible on which of those assumes primacy at any time. The government and RBI need to soften their respective stances and come up with workable solutions; it is incumbent upon both to ensure there is no more rancor. On issues of operational autonomy, the government needs to lay off its pressure on the RBI. On macro issues such as exchange rate management and RBI's dividend policy, written agreements that clearly demarcate roles and re-sponsibilities can be thrashed out. For the health of India's economy and institutions, the contingencies of politics must not be allowed to over-rule the demands of fiscal and monetary prudence. The Monetary Policy

Framework Agreement and the FRBM Act are good illustrations of how a mutually agreed rule-based framework can broker peace between the central bank and the executive arm of government.[6] Former RBI Governor Y.V. Reddy in his autobiography "Advice and Dissent" opined that RBI is independent but within the limits set by the government. There are enough mechanisms within the government system to resolve these.[7]

The controversy over the RBI's independence cloaks a bigger issue: the government's chronic inability to control overspending and the fiscal deficit. Existential conflicts between the RBI and government had caused stress in the system. Contentious issues are always there but they should not lead to the Governor resigning. The most independent central bank is not likely to be a socially optimal central bank. The biggest lesson from the global financial crisis was cooperation between the monetary and fiscal policy authorities is crucial for growth and stability of the economy. RBI needs autonomy. But government also has its fair share of responsibilities. The central bank must also be sometimes sensitive to an elected government's concerns, especially when systemic issues like credit market operations may be at stake. That's what democracy is, also, about.[8]

## Endnotes

1. Evolving Role of the Reserve Bank of India: Recent Developments Y.V. Reddy, RBI Bulletin, December 2007.

2. Lok Sabha Secretariat. 2013. "Financial Sector in India: Regulations and Reforms," Reference Notes, No. 15 /RN/Ref./August/2013. http://164.100.47.193/intranet/financialsectorinindia.pdf, (accessed October 20, 2018).

3. R. Sarin. November 9, 2018. "Two Years after Demonetisation: Okaying Note Ban, RBI Rejected Govt Caim on Black Money, Fake Notes." *The Indian Express*. https://indianexpress.com/article/india/two-years-after-demonetisation-okaying-note-ban-rbi-rejected-govt-claim-on-black-money-fake-notes-5438516/, (accessed March 6, 2019).

4. Foreword in a book "Demonetization and Black Money" by C. Rammanohar Reddy, Orient Black Swan, Hyderabad, India, 2017.

5. Cease Fire, Editorial Comment, *The Indian Express*, November 1, 2018.

6. At loggerheads, Editorial comment, *The Hindu Business Line*, October 30, 2018.

7. RBI can't Claim Complete Autonomy: PMEAC's Bibek Debroy, News Headline, *MINT*, November 2, 2018.

8. Cordial Tête-à-Têtes for Entente Cordiale, Editorial Comment, *The Economic Times*, November 1, 2018.

# CHAPTER 14

# The Ongoing Debate and Political Economy

Demonetization was a decision with few parallels in India's economic history. It was both an economic and a political necessity. The government's aspirations for India are important. It can be seen as more than an economic policy, rather as a political tool. Modi has staked his position as a leader capable of making bold decisions. The unprecedented boldness of the decision itself seems, at least in urban and semi-urban India, to have played in his favor. It seems the government has successfully portrayed support for demonetization as a civic and patriotic duty, using paternalistic messaging and repeated assurances that the end justifies the means (Beyes and Bhattacharya 2017). It has reinvigorated the Indian public debate about black money and corruption. The impact of demonetization is felt by every Indian citizen. The economic history is a harsh and unforgiving judge. What counts in the end is success measured in terms of the stated goals of the policy.

Right from the moment demonetization was announced, the prime minister acknowledged that peoples' lives would be disrupted. He invoked civic duty and patriotism: Citizens should accept the challenges of demonetization as a "sacrifice" and "face difficulties for the benefit of the nation." This appeal to the greater common good permeates the prime minister's speeches on demonetization, culminating in his New Year address, in which he compared the "patience, discipline, and resolve" that the past seven and a half weeks had required to wars that India had fought in previous decades. Like soldiers fighting external threats, citizens should "unite to fight a war against [the] internal evils" of corruption, black money, and counterfeit notes. The flipside of this argument, of course, is that critics and opponents of demonetization lack patriotism (Beyes and Bhattacharya 2017).

## Political Economy in the Era of Post-Truth

"Post-truth" is defined as "relating to or denoting circumstances in which objective facts are less influential in shaping public opinion than appeals to emotion and personal belief."[1] In this context, truth, meaning a description of the world as it really is, has ceased to be important. Once corruption has evolved in the imagination of the people as big scams, and once people are made to believe corrupt accumulations of black money are hidden in piles of currency, the truth of describing that spurt in corruption scams was sparked by the reforms and that much of what is accumulated as black money is hardly kept in cash does not seem to matter much to the people at large. It is on this post-truth "reality" that the government built up its political strategy of destroying corruption and black money with demonetization. Demonetization is a political gamble, but one that a country like India had to take. Critics were overly obsessed with the financial and economic impact of demonetization and neglected to pay adequate attention to the political design underlying it. It has been pointed out that there are three significant aspects one can observe in the government's political narrative:

I. The moralization of politics,
II. The infusion of emotion into policy debates, and
III. The reduction of all debate to a single question.

Whether one likes it or not, the vulnerability lies in the possible parallel that the "demonetization story" holds to the ongoing "nationality story" of the government. It is interesting to note that the government believed in making decisions that were good for people, not those that people would like. There is no greater political danger than constructing an image, making the people believe in it, and riding on those beliefs (Reddy 2017b).

## Problems of Tracking the Black Money

There are organizations and people in India who have access to money-laundering networks and creative schemes for getting around rules and regulations. Almost 99 percent of demonetized currency had been returned to the banking system. In countries where the writ of law is not binding on the rich and influential, there is a tendency to defy the obligation to document financial transactions and pay taxes. As such, demonetization seems to be a case of major strategic fault because instead of collecting the tax in advance, the government is now chasing the black money to collect taxes.

The most interesting point in discussion is "black money and politics." The reason why the political opposition's criticism against demonetization carried no weight is its reluctance to talk about black money and politics. Also, over the years, the greater use of black money in politics has been linked with wealthier candidates contesting elections as they have a greater chance of winning. The biggest demand for cash is from electioneering politicians. The practice of political parties mopping up a large amount of election funds through unaccounted contributions pushes businesses to generate black money. Civil servants allegedly get involved too, making them corrupt. Reddy (2017b) makes a perceptive point of the winning candidates' exponential growth in assets while in office. Coalition Partners insistence for more "lucrative portfolios" as the money "invested" fighting the elections has to be recouped while in office. Electoral politics has also been shaped by these hoards of money. The government had claimed the mantle of anti-corruption. Demonetization has come as a shock and awe for the political parties and politicians for whom black money is a lifeline and will help make the election process clean and transparent. But it has brought tough times for the political parties and politicians who believe in the idea of purchasing votes in exchange for notes.

Some positive impact is visible on the political front. The government announced an electoral funding reform, including a reduction in the permissible amounts of anonymous political donations by a factor of 10, from ₹ 20,000 to ₹ 2,000. Such measures to institutionalize political funding have been long-standing recommendations of the Election Commission of India (EC) to address corruption in the electoral process. The announcement sent a positive message *vis-a-vis* the integrity of the demonetization exercise and the government's commitment to address the primary roots of corruption more broadly (Beyes and Bhattacharya 2017). Predicting the future is difficult; it is yet to be seen how this reform impacts the nexus between elections and corruption in the long run. As per Moody's, demonetization will strengthen India's institutional framework by reducing tax avoidance and corruption. It would result in efficiency gains through greater formalization of economic and financial activity, which would help broaden the tax base and expand usage of the financial system.[2]

While digital transactions did spike post-demonetization (when consumers had few alternatives), one must rely on an understanding of factors that drive digital adoption as digital uptake has the prospect to deliver over the longer term. The economy would also be serviced by both cash and highly digitized transactions. In spite of challenges, public reactions to demonetization were initially broadly positive. The policy's perceived decisiveness struck a chord with the electorate. Political analysts feel that people of the country had supported the union government's intent to act against black money, and the electoral success in Uttar Pradesh was an example of the support for the decision. It appeared there was a consensus that innovative, perhaps radical anti-corruption, policies were needed and that this consensus was so strong it outweighed even personal inconvenience and potential economic losses (Beyes and Bhattacharya 2017). Overall, the biggest hope of long-term payoffs for the economy lies in forcing a behavioral change on tax evaders. It not only changed the agenda and made corruption difficult, but because it was a "morally and ethically correct" step, it was also "politically correct" (Mathew 2017).

## Uncertainty of Long-Term Impact

The targeted benefits of demonetization would be in the long run. How long is not very clear. Only time will tell. Rakshit (2018) is of the view that the long-run impact of a one-off demonetization is unlikely to be significant or unambiguous. The net results of the cost–benefit calculus are not so clear-cut. A worthwhile research program is expected to shed new light not only on the consequences of demonetization but also on the working of the Indian economy in response to other important policies and events. The short-term pains to demonetization are acknowledged. The failure of the government lies not only in the demonetization exercise but also in the failure to grapple seriously with the inefficiencies that inhere in the Indian economy. Farmers' distress has gone national, as has the demand for waiving loans given to farmers. The resulting fiscal burden on states is a cost of the note ban exercise.

The policy of demonetization was a bold political and economic experiment. The Economic Survey (2016 to 2017) seeks to discuss "complexities of the analytics, empirics and potential impacts of demonetization." It is difficult to resist the conclusion that the Economic Survey has been used to justify the decision on demonetization and related issues. Counterfeit notes are the result of deficiencies in the currency management architecture of the RBI. It is important for the RBI to improve the currency management architecture. From a longer-term perspective, it is important to strengthen the currency management architecture and tax administration without harassment. Government spokespersons may have been more effective in media debates, but on the economic plane, there has been a glaring lack of trust in the narrative.

Demonetization decision was taken with good intent. But the government is not adequately focused on ensuring growth, job creation, and investment. It put the economy into a spin. Critics of demonetization cite the deceleration of growth. The government is on the defensive because of the slowdown in the economy, and the opposition parties see this as an opening to target the government. But some measure of deceleration was predicted. Unfortunately, there are reasons to believe that other factors, possibly arising due to structural causes and with long-term effects, have also played an important role in slowing down the economy. Stopping and reversing the slowdown call for a multi-sectoral, multi-pronged, multi-government level approach. There won't be one single silver bullet (Ranade 2017).

Mehta (2017) has opined that "demonetization was a populist measure, done in the name of the poor. It hurt them by extracting the highest price from them. It is doubtful that the measure dented the complex webs through which plutocracies shield their money. Indeed, new laundering mechanisms came into being as a result. Demonetization created fantasies of a cashless economy, but cash is back with a vengeance. Formalization was a desirable objective of demonetization. But it underestimated the fact that informality was also a form of low-cost participation. Formalization without preparation leads to exclusion."

Demonetization hit the poor, but they forgave because they believed the government was on their side and the move was aimed against "filthy rich people." It was, however, yet to be known whether the rich got hurt. People were upset with the establishment—the rich people and the government, that is, the crony capitalism. Other people suffering took it as a triumph. The government has obviously used it as a potent political tool and has demonstrated that the measure did not hurt at the political hustings. It is important for the government to now invest its political capital on rebooting the economy. Some of that has been on show recently. However, the political effect on the opposition of their protests has been less than salutary. The demonetization decision could be the first step in rewriting the social contract in India. If the vast majority of people feel their representatives are not delivering, basic rules of social order fall apart as local law enforcement agencies are viewed as corrupt and venal. To reinforce this social contract with the people, the government must take steps that will hurt the fat cats. Only then will it be possible to talk about a new social contract, where citizens feel that paying taxes in return for social services is a good deal (Hyder and Khan 2016).

Policy actions have real consequences, and tracing the path toward their wider impact is difficult and complex. There may be short-term political benefits, but the negative impact on the economy can create longer-term risks and eventually bite back. Such policy ought to be founded on both theory and evidence. India's demonetization should serve as a cautionary tale (Chakravorti 2017). For many Indians, Modi is a beacon of nationalism—a man who binds the country together through his iconic speeches. But for the opposition, he is an authoritarian figure who has made the honest Indian suffer through his sudden decision to remove cash from the economy (Mukhopadhyay 2017). One can view demonetization as removal of distortions that may increase total factor productivity (TFP) and resource allocation in the long run. It would drain the swamp because hoarders have come up with ingenious methods of laundering their money. One may have to pay more attention to the nature of transformation in the public imagination about the notions of black money and corruption. Somehow, adequate attention needs to contextualize the images constructed around black money and corruption and the effective way in which these images were put to political use by the government (Reddy 2017b). A few voices against demonetization remain as loud as ever. The criticism that has the strongest force relates to the badly handled remonetization of the economy. However, the disruption caused by demonetization was needed for the country to move toward a "new normal."

## Endnotes

1. Time. November 16, 2016. "Oxford's Word of the Year for 2016 is 'Post-Truth,'" http://time.com/4572592/oxford-word-of-the-year-2016-post-truth, (accessed October 17, 2017).
2. Demonetization Credit Positive as it will Cut Tax Avoidance, Corruption: Moody's, News Headline, *The Hindu Business Line*, March 1, 2017.

# CHAPTER 15

# An Epilogue: Two Years Later

There has been a renewed debate around demonetization on its second anniversary; the government and the opposition attacked each other over its lasting impact. On November 24, 2016, speaking in the Rajya Sabha, a little over 2 weeks after demonetization, former prime minister Manmohan Singh had described it as "organized loot and legalized plunder of the common people." Again, on the second anniversary of demonetization, he asserted that it was an "ill-fated" and "ill-thought" exercise. "Notebandi" impacted every single person, regardless of age, gender, religion, occupation, or creed. He advised the government to show prudence, thought, and care in its handling of economic policy making and urged the government to restore certainty and visibility in economic policies.[1] Critiques view demonetization was devoid of economic rationale. India was not suffering from hyperinflation or loss of faith in its currency calling for a radical recall of notes. The economy, on the contrary, was in fine fettle. Demonetization proved to be just an unnecessary disruptor. More than slowing growth and derailing reforms, demonetization inflicted avoidable pain. Nor did it deal a body blow to black money.[2]

The dishonest had got the better of the government. They invented innumerable ways to deposit their illegal holdings of cash in the banks. But one should not be blind to the fact that the larger part of black money generation now takes place inside and not outside the circuits of the banking system. Nirav Modi and Mehul "Bhai" Choksi looted the banks and transferred wealth through banking channels. It is far too early to claim any transformation in tax revenue collections. In some respects, black money has actually taken steps to facilitate the greater use of black money. Its system of electoral bonds (introduced in 2017 after demonetization) in which the donor is anonymous—and can, therefore, call in favors after an election—is designed for corruption (Reddy 2018).

The government did not celebrate the second anniversary of demonetization. The finance minister did come out with a statement listing the achievements of demonetization. He made a valiant defense of demonetization. According to him, an ill-informed criticism of demonetization is that almost the entire cash money got deposited in the banks. The objective was digitalization, better tax compliance, and "formalization" of the economy. The system required to be shaken in order to make India move from cash to digital transactions. This would obviously have an impact on higher tax revenue and a higher tax base.[3] The increase in tax revenues after demonetization does not justify such a large-scale disruption.

Demonetization led to considerable uncertainty increase in the economy. Experiments in macroeconomic policy like India's demonetization are rare. One has to make a decision, which requires guts and courage; right or wrong is a different thing. A moment comes in the nation's history when some harsh and unpleasant decisions are to be made. Every policy has a stated goal as well as secondary consequences, some of which are unintended. The implementation was a bit haphazard, everyone agrees with that. It seems that the government had not anticipated the magnitude of the problem. The enormity of the challenge has brought out the weakness in governance. The inherent limitation of demonetization has to be kept in mind while evaluating it. Political dynamics can be quite different from economic dynamics. Implementation process should not in itself be cast as a blanket indictment of the demonetization strategy.

Demonetization will continue to enliven analysis for a long time to come. A lot has been written and speculated about demonetization since its introduction. Such a large and unexpected policy change naturally carries with it a large collateral damage at least in the short run. Intellectuals and analysts have slammed the step. The economics and politics of demonetization bear no connection, with the idea of finding favor with citizens by virtue of the populist appeal of its moral logic. Demonetization is a perfect example of one such impactful socioeconomic change. Despite the hardships people faced, economic activity continued, growth happened, and corporate profits grew. The stoic manner in which ordinary Indians were willing to be part of an economic and social experiment requires deeper sociological analysis (Baru 2017). In some surveys, it was found that people felt the pleasure from thinking about corrupt politicians suffering losses and most negatively affected by the demonetization than farmers and workers. Ironically, it does not appear that the "corrupt rich" lost too much.[4] But it is not clear whether the people, in general, understand this, and the result is far from definitive.

Demonetization's worst effects on the economy are a thing of the past now. Benefits of digitalization are a slow natural process. India cannot leapfrog advanced economies and get there by a policy intervention like demonetization. The most basic thing is the stability of the money supply. There is a tendency for people to hold on to high currency notes. Looking at the currency in circulation, the ₹ 2,000 note, few want to hold as a medium of exchange but many might want as a store of value. In other words, it would have high demand, but low velocity (the rate at which it is transacted). The ₹ 200 note is more liquid. Demonetization may be a tool for rebalancing currency circulation, including mix of higher and lower denomination notes. It is not known what the ideal combination should be, but it is in the realm of the government and the RBI to have some sense of intelligence of these dynamics. There may be more currency circulating now than on the eve of demonetization, but India's nominal GDP is far higher. The transactions demand for cash is related to income. If income (GDP) increases, cash demand also increases. In the 11 quarters since pre-demonetization (September 2016 to September 2018), cash has increased by 8.3 percent; and nominal GDP is estimated to have increased by 23 percent; that is a cash-income elasticity of one-third the historical average. This shows that demonetization had an impact on cash demand (Bhalla 2018). But while viewing cash as bad, one should not forget the fact that it drives a large part of the economy.

One cannot see the demonetization move in isolation—this is part of the larger design to unearth black money. Any method to curb black money will have a certain amount of uncertainty associated with it. There is no perfect method. There are lakhs of suspicious transactions where people have deposited large amount of cash with banks, which their financial background does not justify; the investigative agencies will get into action and track down these people. People with black money now know that they are under scanner. Controlling black money is in the nature of work in progress.

One should also need to take into consideration the rise in cashless transactions. Digital payments have risen sharply and become commonplace, which testifies to the significant impact of demonetization on increasing such transactions. Two years after demonetization, retail digital payments have soared. Retail digital transactions include paper clearing or checks; retail electronic clearing, such as NEFT (national electronic funds transfer), IMPS (immediate payment service), and card transactions that happen at Point of Sale (PoS), including online transactions pre-paid instruments (PPIs); and mobile banking. Almost every single instrument of digital transaction has shown a phenomenal increase. The increase in digital transactions, taken together with the introduction of the GST, will also have the effect of increasing the size of the formal economy and reducing that of the informal economy. It has improved transmission in the banking system and led to the greater financialization of savings. But digitization does not necessarily check black income generation.

Whoever expects that the demonetization process will be a great success is mistaken. The ongoing battle over demonetization appears to be waged more in the social media and between politicians than in the public imagination. That demonetization has and will continue to have many enemies is undeniable. The significant political connections of the black economy also meant that all attempts to ensure better compliance through a combination of incentives and threats inevitably failed to achieve the desired results. The discourse always favored a show of political will, and there was always a lament that this would never be forthcoming (Dasgupta 2018).

Demonetization has raised more questions than it has answered. The difficulty in making a cost–benefit analysis is that the demonetization move was not purely economic. It would be fair to say the intent was good. But certainly at this point, one still cannot in any way say it has been an economic success. Several other supportive measures are required by the government to change the economy for good. Moreover, it is critical to emphasize that demonetization was a unique event, and hence, drawing inferences based on theory, armchair analysis, or even short-term data could lead to misleading conclusions. Serious research needs to be done extremely carefully, and reasonably long-term data must be considered before reaching any conclusion about unprecedented policy events such as demonetization. It will probably take several years before the outcomes can be evaluated with analytical rigor. This becomes even more important when there are other related moving parts such as GST, clean-up of the banking system, real estate sector reform, and others going on at the same time. So, at the moment, it is better to wait a bit longer until a complete analysis of effects of demonetization is done to reach the correct conclusion. However, demonetization will not produce bad outcomes in the long run.

## Endnotes

1. Scars of Note Ban Getting more Visible with Time, says Manmohan Singh, *Business Standard*, November 9, 2018.
2. Two years Later, Editorial Comment, *The Indian Express*, November 9, 2018.
3. Currency Confiscation was not Objective of Demonetization: Arun Jaitley, *The Indian Express*, November 9, 2018.
4. Banerjee, A., and N. Kala. June 21, 2017. "The Economic and Political Consequences of India's Demonetization," https://voxdev .org/topic/institutions-political-economy/economic-and-political-consequences-india-s-demonetization, (accessed October 31, 2018).

# References

Bakshi, I. December 4, 2017. "Demand-supply Shock Debate Divides Economists Growth Story," *Business Standard*. https://www.business-standard.com/article/economy-policy/demand-supply-shock-debate-divides-economists-117120300559_1.html, (accessed January 15, 2019).

Baru, S. November 7, 2017. "Government's Policy Activism Must Continue Even though Jury is Out on its Success," *The Economic Times*. https://economictimes.indiatimes.com/news/economy/policy/view-governments-policy-activism-must-continue-even-though-jury-is-out-on-its-success/articleshow/61535637.cms, (accessed January 15, 2019).

Behl, V. October 28, 2017. "Demonetisation was Blessing for Realty Sector, RERA & GST will Clean it Up," *Business Standard*. https://www.business-standard.com/article/economy-policy/demonetisation-was-blessing-for-realty-sector-rera-gst-will-clean-it-up-117102800265_1.html, (accessed January 15, 2019).

Beyes, P., and R. Bhattacharya. 2017. "India's 2016 Demonetisation Drive: A Case Study on Innovation in Anti-corruption Policies, Government Communications and Political Integrity." https://www.oecd.org/cleangovbiz/Integrity-Forum-2017-Beyes-Bhattacharya-India-demonetisation-drive.pdf, (accessed August 14, 2018).

Beyer, R. C. M., E. Chhabra, V. Galdo, and M. Rama. 2018. Measuring Districts' Monthly Economic Activity from Outer Space. World Bank, WPS8523, Volume no. 1. https://openknowledge.worldbank.org/bitstream/handle/10986/29996/WPS8523.pdf?sequence=1&isAllowed=y, (accessed January 15, 2019).

Bhagwati, J., V. Dehejia, and P. Krishna. December 27, 2016. "Demonetisation Fallacies and Demonetisation Math," *MINT*. https://www.livemint.com/Opinion/niFH9uM377oUSHEQcRuUWP/Demonetisation-fallacies-and-demonetisation-math.html, (accessed January 15, 2019).

Bhalla, S. S. November 10, 2018. "MoF and RBI Examining the Divide," *Financial Express*. https://www.financialexpress.com/opinion/examining-the-mof-and-rbi-divide-do-high-real-interest-rates-hurt-a-fast-growing-economy-and-the-people/1377507, (accessed January 15, 2019).

Butani, M. November 30, 2016. "Demonetisation Decoded: Time to Embrace a Cashless Economy; Global Trend Moving that Way Demonetisation, GDP, Cashless Economy, Indian Economy," *The Financial Express*. https://www.financialexpress.com/opinion/demonetisation-decoded-time-to-embrace-a-cashless-economy-global-trend-moving-that-way-demonetisation-gdp-cashless-economy-indian-economy/459780, (accessed January 15, 2019).

Chakravorti, B. November 2, 2017. "One Year after India Killed off Cash, Here's What Other Countries Should Learn from it." https://hbr.org/2017/11/one-year-after-india-killed-off-cash-heres-what-other-countries-should-learn-from-it, (accessed August 19, 2018).

Chanda, A. December 17, 2016. "Notes (and anecdotes) on Demonetisation." https://sites01.lsu.edu/faculty/achanda/wp-content/uploads/sites/136/2016/12/Notes-on-Demonetization.pdf, (accessed August 19, 2018).

Chengappa, R. December 29, 2016. "Interview of the Year: PM Narendra Modi exclusive, his First Since Demonetisation," *India Today*, (with Group Editorial Director). https://www.indiatoday.in/magazine/cover-story/story/20170109-narendra-modi-black-money-demonetisation-opposition-830098-2016-12-29, (accessed January 15, 2019).

Dasgupta, D. September 11, 2018. "Demonetisation: The Good, the Bad and the Ugly," *The Telegraph*. https://www.telegraphindia.com/opinion/balancing-columns/cid/1667326, (accessed January 15, 2019).

Dasgupta, S. November 13, 2018. "Modi doesn't Shy Away from Long Term Issues," *The Free Press Journal*. https://m.dailyhunt.in/news/india/english/the+free+press+journal-epaper-fpressjr/modi+doesn+t+shy+away+from+lon g+term+issues-newsid-101371562, (accessed January 15, 2019).

Deodhar, S. Y. November 8, 2017. "Demonetisation and the Fight against Black Money," *MINT*. https://www.livemint.com/Opinion/sH5FSnXPkuAh-knhzuPgH3M/Demonetisation-and-the-fight-against-black-money.html, (accessed January 15, 2019).

Dominic, B. January 19, 2017. "Making Indians Shift to Cashless Transactions," *MINT*. https://www.livemint.com/Opinion/HkDJ0D2pJvQls1H4KMGUPN/Making-Indians-shift-to-cashless-transactions.html, (accessed January 15, 2019).

Doctor, V. November 12, 2016. "The Cycles of Demonetisation: A Looks Back at Two Similar Experiments in 1946 and 1978," *The Economic Times*. https://economictimes.indiatimes.com/blogs/onmyplate/the-cycles-of-demonetisa-tion-a-looks-back-at-two-similar-experiments-in-1946-and-1978, (accessed January 15, 2019).

Einzig, P. 1959. *How Money is Managed*. Baltimore, MA: Penguin Books Inc.

Fernandes, F., and S. Sukhi. December 18, 2016. "Over 9,000 crores Deposited in District Co-operative Banks in 5 Days Post Demonetisation," *The Economic Times*. https://economictimes.indiatimes.com/industry/banking/finance/bank-ing/over-rs-9000-crore-deposited-in-district-co-op-banks-in-5-days-post-de-monetisation/articleshow/56046062.cms, (accessed January 15, 2019).

Froyen, R. T. 2009. *Macroeconomics: Theories and Policies*. 8th ed. New Delhi, India: Pearson Education.

Ghosh, S. October 4, 2018. "Indians Shunned One-two Year Term Deposits dur-ing Demonetization: Report," *MINT*. https://www.livemint.com/Politics/

quZDTMD2Q5f10vYYMLmywL/Indians-shunned-onetwo-year-term-deposits-during-demonetiza.html, (accessed January 16, 2019).

Ghosh, T. P. November 21, 2017. "Efficacy of Demonetisation in Eliminating Black Money an Analysis of Indian Demonetisation November 2016." *Journal of Management and Strategy* 8, no. 5. http://www.sciedu.ca/journal/index.php/jms/article/view/12583/7754, (accessed January 15, 2019).

Government of India (GoI). 2012. *White Paper on Black Money*. New Delhi, India: Ministry of Finance. http://www.prsindia.org/uploads/media/White%20Paper%20Black%20Money/WhitePaper_BackMoney2012.pdf, (accessed January 15, 2019).

Ghandy, K. 2016. "Demonetisation: One Step Forward, Two Steps Back." *Economic and Political Weekly*, 51, no. 50. https://www.epw.in/system/files/pdf/2016_51/50/Demonetisation_0.pdf, (accessed January 15, 2019).

Gupta, K. May 26, 2018. "Banking Sector in 4 Years of Modi Govt: Note Ban Sets off Surge in Digital Transactions," *MINT*. https://www.livemint.com/Politics/1VvHw5o828Ou9cFbpnDVcL/Banking-sector-in-4-years-of-Modi-govt-Note-ban-sets-off-su.html, (accessed January 15, 2019).

Gurumurthy, S. September 5, 2017. "De-mon—A Multidimensional Project," *The Indian Express*. http://www.newindianexpress.com/opinions/columns/s-gurumurthy/2017/sep/05/de-mon--a-multidimensional-project-1652562.html, (accessed January 15, 2019).

Hattangadi, A., and S. Kelkar. March 15, 2017. "The Narrative in Post-demonetized India," *MINT*. https://www.livemint.com/Opinion/ge3VqC-mlfkOvz8PHr06MZN/The-narrative-in-postdemonetised-India.html, (accessed January 15, 2019).

Hyder, D., and M. Khan. December 19, 2016. "India's Demonetization: Have Policymakers Lost their Minds?" *Herald Dawn*. https://herald.dawn.com/news/1153608, (accessed September 10, 2018).

Kamath, S. November 16, 2016. "Unknown Facts about Demonetization 1946, 1978 and 2016." http://awordtotheworld.com/unknown-facts-about-demonetization-1946-1978-and-2016, (accessed August 20, 2018).

Kapadia, A. 2016. "Money and 'Demonetisation.'" *Economic and Political Weekly* 51, no. 51. https://www.epw.in/system/files/pdf/2016_51/51/PE_LI_51_171216_Anush_Kapadia.pdf, (accessed January 15, 2019).

Kapoor, D. December 20, 2016. "Demonetisation—The Long and Short of It." http://www.forbesindia.com/blog/economy-policy/demonetisation-the-long-and-short-of-it, (accessed September 15, 2018).

Kinger, D. September 2, 2016. "The Many Virtues of E-cash," *The Hindu Business Line*. https://www.thehindubusinessline.com/opinion/the-many-virtues-of-ecash/article9060939.ece, (accessed January 15, 2019).

Kohli, R. November 22, 2016. "Demonetization: The Impact on Agriculture," *MINT*. http://www.livemint.com/Opinion/B1vFTOgwqHjdM5nkmg2CxJ /Demonetization-The-impact-on-agriculture.html, (accessed January 15, 2019).

Kohli, R. September 5, 2018. "Defend Demonetisation, but at Least Sound Credible," *Financial Express*. https://www.financialexpress.com/opinion/ defend-demonetisation-but-at-least-sound-credible/1302893, (accessed January 15, 2019).

Kumar, A. P. 2016a. "Demonetisation and the Rule of Law," *Economic and Political Weekly* 51, no. 50. https://www.epw.in/system/files/pdf/2016_51/50/ CM_LI_50_101216_Alok%20Prasanna%20Kumar.pdf, (accessed January 15, 2019).

Kumar, A. 2016b. "Estimation of the Size of the Black Economy in India, 1996–2012," *Economic Political Weekly* 51, no. 48. https://www.epw.in/system/ files/pdf/2016_51/48/Estimation_of_the_Size_of_the_Black_Economy_ in_India%2C_1996-2012_0.pdf, (accessed January 15, 2019).

Kumar, A. August 20, 2011. "The Cost of the Black Economy," *The Hindu*. https://www.thehindu.com/opinion/lead/the-cost-of-the-black-economy/ article2373664.ece, (accessed January 16, 2019).

Lahiri, A. K. December 2016. Demonetization, the Cash Shortage and the Black Money, National Institute of Public Finance and Policy, Working Paper No. 184, New Delhi, India. http://nipfp.org.in/media/medialibrary/2016/12/ WP_2016_184.pdf, (accessed September 15, 2018).

Lenz, G. S. 2012. *"Follow the Leader? How Voters Respond to Politicians' Policies and Performance* (Chicago Studies in American Politics)." Chicago, IL: University of Chicago Press.

Mathew, L. November 8, 2017. "Note Ban Ethical, Moral Decision: Arun Jaitley," *The Indian Express*. https://indianexpress.com/article/india/post-demonetisa- tion-note-ban-ethical-moral-decision-arun-jaitley, (accessed January 16, 2019).

Mehta, P. B. November 8, 2017. "Revolution that wasn't," *The Indian Express*. https://indianexpress.com/article/opinion/columns/demonetisation-pm-modi- notes-ban-one-year-of-demonetisation-4927169, (accessed January 16, 2019).

Mirchandani, S. January 5, 2017. "MSME Sector Growth to be Muted due to Demonetisation: Crisil," *The Economic Times*. https://economic- times.indiatimes.com/small-biz/sme-sector/msme-sector-growth-to-be- muted-due-to-demonetiation-crisil/articleshow/56357012.cms, (accessed January 16, 2019).

Mishra, A. December 5, 2016. "Demonetisation: Everything You Need to Know!" https://www.linkedin.com/pulse/everything-you-need-know-de- monetisation-ashish-mishra, (accessed September 24, 2018).

Mukherjee, S. May 25, 2018. "Demonetization a Big Boon," *DNA.* https://www
    .dnaindia.com/analysis/column-demonetization-a-big-boon-2618497, (accessed
    January 16, 2019).

Mukhopadhyay, A. January 16, 2017. "Demonetization: Modi's Triumph or His
    Biggest Failure?" https://www.fairobserver.com/region/central_south_asia/de-
    monetization-india-narendra-modi-news-analysis-34034, (accessed January 16,
    2019).

Nanavati, U. January 3, 2017. "At Crossroads: MSMEs Feel the Demonetisa-
    tion Squeeze," *The Economic Times.* https://economictimes.indiatimes.com/
    small-biz/sme-sector/at-crossroads-msmes-feel-the-demonetisation-squeeze/
    articleshow/56306520.cms, (accessed January 16, 2019).

Nataraj, G. 2017. "Demonetisation and its Impact," New Delhi: India: Indian
    Institute of Public Administration (IIPA). http://www.iipa.org.in/upload/
    Theme%20Paper%20for%20Members'%20Annual%20Conference%20
    2017.pdf, (accessed September 16, 2018).

Nayak, P. B. March 4, 2017a. "The Anatomy of Black Money," *The Indian
    Express.* https://indianexpress.com/article/lifestyle/books/the-anatomy-of-
    black-money-narendra-modi-demonetisation-shankar-acharya-arun-kumar-
    avl-narayana-and-raja-chelliah-the-black-economy-cambridge-economist-
    nicholas-kaldo-wanchoo-committee-report-4553191, (accessed January 16,
    2019).

Nayak, P. B. April 17, 2017b. "Show Me the Money," *The Indian Express.* https://
    indianexpress.com/article/opinion/columns/ban-on-rs-500-rs-1000-notes-
    pm-modi-black-money-cashless-economy-4368777, (accessed January 16,
    2019).

Nayyar, D. December 9, 2016. "Demonetisation: Politics Trumps Economics,"
    *MINT.* https://www.livemint.com/Opinion/Pt92dQonYDzCgn8itvIrnK/
    Demonetisation-Politics-trumps-economics.html, (accessed January 16,
    2019).

Newlyn, W. T. 1978. *Theory of Money.* London, UK: Oxford University Press.

OECD. 2016. "2017 OECD Global Anti-Corruption Integrity Forum, Beyes,
    and Bhattacharya's, paper was submitted as part of a competitive call for
    papers on integrity, anti-corruption and inclusive growth in the context of
    the 2017 OECD Global Anti-Corruption & Integrity Forum." https://www
    .oecd.org/cleangovbiz/Integrity-Forum-2017-Beyes-Bhattacharya-India-de-
    monetisation-drive.pdf, (accessed January 16, 2019)

Padmanabhan, V. August 30, 2018. "From GDP Growth to Black Money, Costs
    Outweigh Benefits of Demonetization," *MINT.* https://www.livemint.com/
    Industry/G0nNMoXXS8eVmW1oqUa1TP/Demonetisation-has-impacted-
    GDP-growth-to-black-money.html, (accessed January 10, 2019).

Pandit, A. 2016. "On the Margins of Society, Demonetisation Haunts Them." http://timesofindia.indiatimes.com/city/delhi/On-the-margins-of-society-emonetisation-hauntsthem/articleshow/55423184.cms, (accessed September 10, 2018).

Patel, I. G. 2002. Glimpses of Indian Economic Policy. New Delhi, India: Oxford University Press.

Patibandla, M., and A. Sanyal. October 2005. "Corruption: Market Reform and Technology." https://www.researchgate.net/publication/256034664_Corruption_Market_Reform_and_Technology, (accessed September 18, 2018).

Rajakumar, J. D., and S. L. Shetty. November 26, 2016. "Demonetisation: 1978, the Present and the Aftermath." *Economic & Political Weekly* 51, no. 48. https://www.epw.in/system/files/pdf/2016_51/48/Demonetisation%3A_1978%2C_the_Present_and_the_Aftermath_0.pdf, (accessed January 16, 2019).

Rajwade, A. V. November 30, 2016. "Achievement, with Some Chinks," *Business Standard*. https://www.business-standard.com/article/opinion/the-calm-before-the-storm-116113001409_1.html, (accessed January 16, 2019).

Rakshit, M. March 31, 2018. "Some Analytics of Demonetisation." *Economic & Political Weekly* 53, no. 13. https://www.epw.in/journal/2018/13/money-banking-and-finance/some-analytics-demonetisation.html, (accessed January 16, 2019).

Ramesh, M. August 31, 2018. "Defending DeMo," *The Hindu Business Line*. https://www.thehindubusinessline.com/opinion/columns/from-the-views-room/defending-demo/article24822143.ece, (accessed January 16, 2019).

Ranade, A. September 18, 2017. "No Silver Bullet for Stopping Economy," *The Free Press Journal*. https://www.freepressjournal.in/editorspick/ajit-ranade-no-silver-bullet-for-stopping-economy/1138867, (accessed January 16, 2019).

Ranade, A. November 2, 2018. "RBI's Independence Needs to be Protected," *MINT*. https://www.livemint.com/Opinion/HL4p6aqH2A30IcTWCAOtjO/Opinion--RBIs-independence-needs-to-be-protected.html, (accessed January 16, 2019).

Rangarajan, C. June 9, 2017. "Getting Back on the Growth Track," *The Hindu*. https://www.thehindu.com/opinion/lead/getting-back-on-the-growth-track/article18868324.ece, (accessed January 16, 2019).

Rao, K., S. Mukherjee, S. Kumar, S. Suranjali Tandon, and S. H. Nayudu. November 14, 2016. Demonetisation: Impact on the Economy, Working Paper No. 182, NIPFP, New Delhi, https://www.nipfp.org.in/media/medialibrary/2016/11/WP_2016_182.pdf, (accessed August 10, 2018).

Rastogi, S. December 22, 2016. "Demonetization: From History to Geography," *DNA*. https://www.dnaindia.com/business/report-demonetization-from-history-to-geography-2285269, (accessed January 16, 2019).

Reddy, C. R. 2017a. *Demonetization and Black Money*. Hyderabad, India: Orient Black Swan.

Reddy, D. N. November 24, 2017b. "In Analysis of the Unfolding Dangers of Opportunistic Politics in the Era of Post-truth," *Frontline*. https://frontline .thehindu.com/migration_catalog/article23773919.ece/BINARY/Full%20 text%20of%20lecture, (accessed January 16, 2019).

Reddy, C. R. November 6, 2018. "Black Hole of Silence on Demonetization," *MINT*. https://www.livemint.com/Politics/uq9SyrATVdQNjDCeas8dnM/ Black-hole-of-silence-on-demonetization.html, (accessed January 18, 2019).

Ritter, L. S., W. L. Silber, and G. F. Udell. 1986. *Principles of Money, Banking and Financial Markets*. 5th ed. New York, NY: Basic Books, Inc., Chapters 1 and 2.

Robertson, D. H. 1922. *Money*. New York, NY: Harcourt Brace and Company.

Rogoff, K. 2016. "India's Currency Exchange and the Curse of Cash." http:// blog.press.princeton.edu/2016/11/17/kenneth-rogoff-indias-currency-exchange-and-the-curse-of-cash, (accessed August 20, 2018).

Roy, A. August 11, 2017. "Demonetisation Effect: RBI's Dividend to Govt Halves to Rs. 30,659 Crore," *Business Standard*. https://www.business-standard.com/ article/economy-policy/demonetisation-effect-rbi-s-dividend-to-govt-halves-to-rs-30-659-crore-117081001540_1.html, (accessed January 16, 2019).

Sabhlok, S. November 22, 2016. "Thoughts on Economics and Liberty." https:// www.sabhlokcity.com/2016/11/a-background-paper-on-black-money-chas-ing-black-money-in-india-by-kishore-c-samal-journal-of-indian-school-of-political-economy-april-june-1992, (accessed October 11, 2018).

Samuelson, P., and W. Nordhaus. 2010. *Economics*. 19th ed. New Delhi, India: McGraw Hill Education.

Sarin, R., J. Mazoomdaar, S. Singh, S. Yadav, and P. V. Iyer. November 7, 2017. "Paradise Papers: Biggest Data Leak Reveals Trails of India's Corporates in Global Secret Tax Havens," *The Indian Express*. https://indianexpress.com/ article/india/paradise-papers-indian-corporates-black-money-4923999, (accessed January 16, 2019).

Sarin, R. November 9, 2018. "Two Years after Demonetization: Okaying Note Ban, RBI Rejected Govt Claim on Black Money, Fake Notes," *The Indian Express*. https://indianexpress.com/article/india/two-years-after-demonetisation-okaying-note-ban-rbi-rejected-govt-claim-on-black-money-fake-notes-5438516, (accessed January 16, 2019).

Sayers, R. S. 1938. *Modern Banking*. London, UK: Oxford University Press.

Sen, A. November 28, 2016. "Both Sides of the Coin: What Top Economists Think about Demonetization." *The Indian Express*. https://indianexpress.com/ article/india/india-news-india/both-sides-of-the-coin-what-top-economists-think-about-demonetisation, (accessed January 16, 2019).

Singh, B. November 2017. "Impact of Demonetisation on the Financial Sector," *RBI Bulletin*, https://rbidocs.rbi.org.in/rdocs/Bulletin/PDFs/IDFS5EBBDC-CB9C274F0E921997DA8EC93CCA.PDF, (accessed January 16, 2019).

Singh, M. December 7, 2006. "PM's Address at LSE Asia Forum Conference in Memory of Dr. I.G. Patel," http://pib.nic.in/newsite/erelcontent .aspx?relid=22902, (accessed January 8, 2019).

Singh, P. November 14, 2014. "Four charts to Explain India's Black Money Problem," *MINT.* https://www.livemint.com/Opinion/5f0l7OFddt5hMae4 TD0bFO/Four-charts-to-explain-Indias-black-money-problem.html, (accessed January 16, 2019).

Singhal, R. August 30, 2018. "How Demonetization Affected the Economy," *MINT.* https://www.livemint.com/Politics/uCSwolE7ugfGfuv2O0wWbN/How-de-monetisation-impacted-the-Indian-economy.html, (accessed January 16, 2019).

Thapar, K. 2017. "Demonetisation has Failed to Tackle Black Money." https:// thewire.in/economy/demonetisation-black-money-corruption, (accessed October 11, 2018).

Vembu, V. November 4, 2017. "False Steps," *The Hindu Business Line.* https:// www.thehindubusinessline.com/blink/cover/false-step/article22224512 .ece1, (accessed January 17, 2019).

Vyas, M. October 13, 2018. "Unemployment, Really," *The Indian Express.* https://indianexpress.com/article/opinion/columns/unemployment-really-cmie-surjit-bhalla-demonetisation-job-cuts-5399928, (accessed January 17, 2019).

Unnikrishnan, D. April 13, 2018. "Rajan vs Patel: What did RBI Advise Govt on Demonetisation? Can the Real Central Bank Please Stand up and Answer?" https://www.firstpost.com/business/rajan-vs-patel-what-did-rbi-advise-govt-on-demonetisation-can-the-real-central-bank-please-stand-up-and-answer-4429813.html, (accessed September 11, 2018).

# About the Author

As an academician, **_Shrawan Kumar Singh_** holds experience in teaching, research, and writing, spanning over five and half decades. He has held academic positions at IGNOU (retired as Professor and Director of School of Social Sciences); University of Delhi (ARSD College); Department of Economics, Faculty of Social Sciences, BHU; and Ranchi University (GLA College, Daltonganj). His field of interest pertains to Indian Economic Policy, Business Environment, and International Business. He has a number of publications to his credit in the form of books, articles, and papers in various journals. He has been associated as visiting faculty to the Department of Commerce and Business Studies, University of Delhi; Sri Ram College of Commerce; Jamia Millia Islamia; Management Development Institute (MDI) (Gurgaon); and FORE School of Management New Delhi. He has participated in teleconferencing, audio-video programs, and phone-in-programs of Akashvani, Doordrashan, and other channels. He has been a member of the UGC Committee on Curriculum Development in Economics (2001), which recommended the UGC Model Curriculum in Economics for under- and postgraduate courses. He is a member of academic bodies like Academic Council and Board of Courses of Studies and professional bodies. Recently, he has contributed to the e-PG Pathshala Project of UGC under the NMEICT mission of MHRD, Government of India, as a content writer in the field of business economics.

# Index

# OTHER TITLES FROM THE ECONOMICS AND PUBLIC POLICY COLLECTION

Philip Romero, The University of Oregon and
Jeffrey Edwards, North Carolina A&T State University, *Editors*

- *A Primer on Microeconomics, Second Edition, Volume II: Competition and Constraints* by Thomas M. Beveridge
- *A Primer on Microeconomics, Second Edition, Volume I: Fundamentals of Exchange* by Thomas M. Beveridge
- *A Primer on Macroeconomics, Second Edition, Volume II: Policies and Perspectives* by Thomas M. Beveridge
- *A Primer on Macroeconomics, Second Edition, Volume I: Elements and Principles* by Thomas M. Beveridge
- *Macroeconomics, Second Edition, Volume I* by David G. Tuerck
- *Macroeconomics, Second Edition, Volume II* by David G. Tuerck
- *Economic Renaissance In the Age of Artificial Intelligence* by Apek Mulay
- *Disaster Risk Management: Case Studies in South Asian Countries* by Huong Ha, R. Lalitha S. Fernando, and Sanjeev Kumar Mahajan
- *The Option Strategy Desk Reference: An Essential Reference for Option Traders* by Russell A. Stultz
- *Disaster Risk Management in Agriculture: Case Studies in South Asian Countries* by Huong Ha, Lalitha S. Fernando, and Sanjeev Kumar Mahajan
- *Foreign Direct Investment* by Leena Kaushal

## Announcing the Business Expert Press Digital Library

*Concise e-books business students need for classroom and research*

This book can also be purchased in an e-book collection by your library as

- *a one-time purchase,*
- *that is owned forever,*
- *allows for simultaneous readers,*
- *has no restrictions on printing, and*
- *can be downloaded as PDFs from within the library community.*

Our digital library collections are a great solution to beat the rising cost of textbooks. E-books can be loaded into their course management systems or onto students' e-book readers. The **Business Expert Press** digital libraries are very affordable, with no obligation to buy in future years. For more information, please visit **www.businessexpertpress.com/librarians**. To set up a trial in the United States, please email **sales@businessexpertpress.com**.